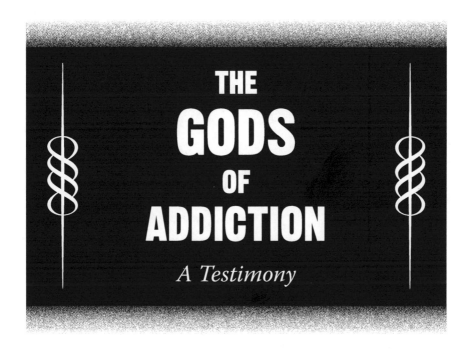

THE
GODS
OF
ADDICTION

A Testimony

CHAPLAIN MITCHELL GREEN

iUniverse, Inc.
Bloomington

The Gods of Addiction
A Testimony

iUniverse books may be ordered through booksellers or by contacting:

iUniverse
1663 Liberty Drive
Bloomington, IN 47403
www.iuniverse.com
1-800-Authors (1-800-288-4677)

ISBN: 978-1-4759-4853-0 (sc)
ISBN: 978-1-4759-4854-7 (e)

Library of Congress Control Number: 2012916334

Printed in the United States of America

iUniverse rev. date: 9/6/2012

This work is dedicated to the sons and daughters of my brothers and sisters, the reigning generation of my family. When I look at your beautiful faces, I see everything that is good and true and pure in the world—everything that God had in mind for His children from the very beginning.

But it grieves me to see deadly temptation knocking at the door of your hearts, grieves me that some of you contemplate opening that door.

Beloved children, I beg of you, stop! Taking that drink, smoking that "blunt," having that sniff of powder may be fashionable and fun, but it comes at a price far greater than it's worth, a price you can spend the rest of your life paying.

I urge you to seek a life free of substance, save for the substance of things hoped for. The substance of faith in Christ Jesus.

Your loving uncle Mitchell

Author's Note

Every day, all over the country and in various other places around the world, millions of men and women struggling with substance addiction find support, strength, and encouragement at AA and NA meetings. I thank God for the inception of these organizations and the service they continue to provide.

Let it be known, therefore, that this work was not written to indict the principles or malign the process employed in the meetings, nor is it my intent to challenge any person, whether layman or professional, actively recovering or active in addiction, who embraces the notion of addiction as a treatable but incurable disease.

I write this to challenge only the notion.

PREFACE

This is a story of demonic possession.

I know—dramatic opening, right? Before beginning this work, I sought the counsel of a friend who suggested my first words should be attention grabbers. As he himself is a writer—recently published and doing fairly well in sales—I considered it sound enough advice.

Man has nursed a lurid and ever-increasing fascination for the subject of demonic possession for as long as he's known he has a spirit to corrupt and a soul to lose. I myself managed to dwell in this life a little over seventeen years before discovering a better than cursory interest in the topic. That was the year that movie was released—you know, the one that featured spirits from hell malevolently taking over an innocent thirteen-year-old girl's body. It was the highest grossing film of its time, enthralling and terrifying movie-goers all over the world. I was newly enlisted in the marines then, only months out of boot camp. I remember sitting in a theater in Fayetteville, North Carolina, with several of my marine buddies trying in all our military intrepidness not to appear schoolgirl-frightened by the sight of Linda Blair mutating, levitating, cursing, spitting, rotating her head 360 degrees, and projectile vomiting all over anyone foolhardy enough to venture within firing range of the bed to which she was strapped. My seventeen-year-old mind thought it was the most obscene idea ever conceived. I was also dissatisfied with the way the girl's ordeal terminated: as inexplicably as it began, after thwarting attempts by all manner of professionals in biology, psychology, and theology (and claiming the lives of two from the last category) to expel the hellish invaders from the body of their hapless adolescent host. I use the term "inexplicably" for two reasons: (1) the pummeling the besieged Miss Blair took at the hands—fists, actually—of Father Karras (one of the two who died) seemed a dubious exorcism technique, its apparent effectiveness notwithstanding; and (2) no clear explanation for the possession was ever given. The story portrayed the victim as the unhappy offspring of divorced parents who were not the best of friends in their separation. Sad, yes, but millions of American kids, myself included, costar in similar stories with no supernatural ramifications. To all appearances—or at least to me—it seemed that the nether creatures had simply chosen a child at random and, after raising hell—or a frightful chunk of it— in her home, simply let her go.

As I said, the movie was a tremendous success and the genre was box-office gold, spawning hundreds of films featuring the malevolent possession not only of humans but of animals and even inanimate objects. From haunted houses to homicidal cars and trucks, to toys with sudden, miraculous mobility and psychotic intent, no person, beast, or thing seemed impervious to spiritual trespass from the astral plane.

No thing and no one, including, as it turned out, me.

This is a story of demonic possession, the spiritual subjugation of a human being—this human being—by living evil. It's not an easy story to tell because while I found the subject entertaining all those years, I was not one to credit its reality. Later, when I came to accept the existence of more things in heaven and on earth than are dreamt of in my philosophy, to paraphrase Shakespeare, I was reluctantly willing to concede the concept as plausible without believing it could apply to me. Even when I was a wrecked and ruined ship tossed about in storm-ravaged waters for thirty years, I never thought to seek out hostile spirits at the heart of my turmoil. To my mind I simply had problems. Problems that broke the hearts of those who loved me most, that mocked and imploded any meaningful relationship to bless my life, and that put a law-abiding society on guard against me. Problems that brought me to the very brink of death and then—unmercifully, I often thought—brought me back.

Even during those rare moments of honest introspection as I considered the erosion of my sanity and deconstruction of my life and admitted something was indeed "wrong with me," I hadn't an inkling what that something was. Not in my most absurd imaginings did the notion that I was a victim of demonic possession occur to me, primarily because I had not seen a single movie or read a book in which possession was shown to be a subtle occurrence. It was always blatant and obvious. While the denizens of the dark realm exploited life issues like social dysfunction, they didn't hide in them. They thrived on and in the limelight and demanded the credit for the destruction they caused. Toward that end, they converted comfortable family homes into refrigerated houses of horror, transformed the lovable family canine into a fanged, bloodthirsty terror, propelled driverless automobiles on murderous rampages, and gave harmless dolls homicidal agendas, knives as long as their bodies gripped in their tiny plastic hands and evil hearts pounding in their plastic chests. With fury and sorcery born of a realm no sane person wants to know about, demons warp and twist the innocent features of thirteen-year-old faces into snarling and lacerated death masks. They endow their victims with the inhuman capacity to endure massive physical trauma without sustaining permanent damage and without a whimper of complaint. The first best evidence of the presence of demonic spirits is the supernatural monstrosities they make of their victims. I could not have known and would not have believed that I myself was such a victim because I underwent no such drastic transformation, nor committed such vile, horrendous acts.

Later I'll recant every word of that.

As I've twice said, this is a story of demonic possession. As you've no doubt gathered from the title, this is also a story about addiction. For more than thirty years these two hellish forces combined and conspired inside me: tearing my life asunder, stretching my sanity to its limit and beyond, and ruining every good thing I ever found, earned, created, or was given. In the following pages I want to share with you my experiences that revealed to me the *persona* of addiction—experiences that exposed addiction as a living, breathing entity, a demon with a dual purpose: to be God to its host and then to kill its host.

This is a story of sickness and insanity, of manipulated will and warped desire, a story of hopelessness, helplessness, and surrender, of twisted, perverted worship masquerading as disease.

This is a story of death and life, a story of the glorious heights to which a soul may rise even after its descent to dark and murky depths. This story is my testimony, a story I should not have survived to write but, because I did survive, *must* write.

This is a story of gods.

And of God.

CHAPTER ONE

I was feeling pretty secure in my sobriety by the time I attended my first recovery meeting outside the Pit Stop. I'd been drug-and-alcohol free for three months after completing the twenty-one-day recovery program and had almost immediately found a job at a company that manufactured zinc dust in East Trenton. It was a tough job. I always came back to my boarding-house room exhausted, filthy, and sore. Despite the paper surgical mask I was required to wear, the gray dust from the ores the company pulverized clung to the hairs in my nostrils. I had to blow until my nose was sore in order to clear out all the debris. But the job paid well, and there was room for advancement. I was already sighting in on a machine or fork-lift operator's position. As I said, I was feeling pretty good. Unless you knew me, you could not have guessed that only a few months prior I had been a cocaine addict for five years—deceitful, desperate, and ready and willing to do whatever it took to feed a habit I had no hope of satisfying.

The program I signed up for was recommended (ordered, actually) by my probation officer. I was twenty-seven and had compiled a fairly extensive criminal record for such crimes as shoplifting, burglary, and possession of controlled substances. The absence of violent offenses in my file had been my only saving grace in terms of avoiding a lengthy prison bid. I once spent forty-five days in the Mercer County Detention Center (in those days known as the "work house") but hadn't come close to doing serious jail time. My probation officer—a smallish, soft-spoken man in his thirties—insisted I go into rehab after I got popped for shoplifting while still on probation, letting me know in no uncertain terms that I would do either the twenty-one-day program or six to nine months in the county lockup for the latest charge.

Richard had been my PO for nearly a year, and this was the first time he ever expressed any real impatience with me. I think he genuinely cared for me, and truthfully I liked him. He always treated me decently, never lording his state-vested authority over me. He was one of those religious types and offered no apologies for it. He was always saying things like "I'm praying for you, Mitch," but he never targeted me with his faith-based rhetoric, and for that I was most appreciative. Not that I was against religion—I practically grew up in church. It's just that religion never got me anywhere. My life remained the same throughout adolescence and into adulthood, so when I was old enough to decide for myself, I decided there were things I'd rather do with my Sunday mornings—like sleep.

But as I said, I liked Richard. He was a good man, so I didn't mind agreeing to the program if it made him happy. Besides, the math—twenty-one days as opposed to six to nine months—pretty much made the decision a no-brainer. On top of that, I reasoned, I needed a little time out of circulation, time to rest and recoup. Cocaine addiction is a rugged life. It revs you full-throttle until you're running out of control. That's why I managed to get myself in trouble while on probation in the first place.

The program was called Project Pit Stop, a name I found ironic for several reasons: (1) the state-run rehab was housed in what was once an auto parts warehouse near a long-abandoned racetrack just outside West Trenton; (2) I was sure the name held biblical applications for Richard, as in stopping me from falling into the pit; and (3) for me this was only a brief respite from the hassle of the hustle—time to recharge my batteries, get a few meals under my belt, clock a few nights' sleep, and lose the ashen pallor my lifestyle had visited upon my complexion. In twenty-two days it would be off to the races again. For me the Pit Stop really was just a pit stop.

There were about twelve staff members at Project Pit Stop, all recovering addicts except for Dr. Berman, the resident psychologist, and Carol, a pretty, light-skinned woman with a really nasty attitude who drove clients (or "inpatients," as we were called) to and from whatever medical or legal appointments were pending. There were forty inpatients, nearly all of us on probation or parole, so someone had to be in one courthouse or another almost every day.

The day started at 6:00. Showers and dorm clean-up until 7:00, and then breakfast until 8:00. Facility chores: cleaning or maintaining offices, meeting rooms, hallways, kitchen, public bathrooms, and grounds until 9:30, and then a short break, after which group meetings were held. To my surprise, I enjoyed the meetings. I found them mildly entertaining at first and then immensely so, and quite moving as well, especially the "sharing," or one person revealing the misadventures of his or her life to a roomful of strangers, speaking to the problems at the heart of one's addiction and then the "feedback" as the sharer's peers offered their opinions or advice about what was shared. It fascinated me to watch people expose themselves so unabashedly, withholding not one sordid detail of their junkie lives. We held two such meetings a day. The sharing got to be pretty emotional and the hour almost always ended with at least a portion of the room in tears. As it turns out, though, melancholy is a contagious mood. Midway through the second week I found myself sharing... and crying. I didn't know I was carrying so much emotional baggage until I started talking about it. It felt good to unload, and amazingly the twenty-one-day "sentence" ended sooner than I wanted. On a bright and breezy Tuesday morning in mid-April I was discharged from Project Pit Stop with a certificate of completion to prove I was recovered from drug addiction.

Upon learning I had completed rehab my mother took me right in. I hadn't seen her during the last few months prior to my most recent arrest. It broke her heart to see me strung out and hustling; overcome with shame, I avoided North Trenton and her house as best I could. Now, however, I was feeling spectacular. Project Pit Stop had proved a more effective experience than I'd anticipated, and I felt as though I really had put down drugs for good. I hadn't even smoked a cigarette in eight days. Truly I was in recovery.

I promised Mom I'd look for a job right away. Two days later I was hired at Federated Metals, and six weeks after that I moved into the boardinghouse in South Trenton. Mom was reluctant to see me go; we'd been sharing some really good times since I got clean, and my sister Brenda didn't care for the area I was moving into. I assured them both I'd be fine. For the first time in more than five years I was thinking about a life that didn't include drugs and alcohol.

Both Alcoholics Anonymous and Narcotics Anonymous meetings were now a condition of my probation, which had been extended another year due to the charge that landed me at Project Pit Stop. The staff at the rehab recommended that I attend a meeting a day for ninety days. I thought that was a bit excessive, and fortunately Richard was willing to settle for three a week. Frankly I wouldn't have been terribly upset if he'd wanted one or two more. Hanging around my room watching television after work had become almost unbearably dull, and there wasn't much else to do since all my former haunts were drug involved. Anyway, I was familiar with meeting protocol because the Pit Stop hosted an AA meeting on Tuesday nights and an NA meeting on Thursday afternoons.

The dining hall in the basement of St. Thomas Church on Chambers Street hosted that night's meeting. There must have been more than three hundred in attendance—easily four times larger than any meeting held at the Pit Stop. I remember wondering if the entire world was in recovery from substance abuse. The atmosphere was light, the general mood cordial. Almost everyone was holding a Styrofoam cup of coffee, and the air was heavy with cigarette breath. I scanned the crowd, guessing every face my gaze fell upon belonged to a smoker. A ticklish surge of superiority swept through me with the thought: I'd beaten drugs *and* cigarettes.

Presently the chairperson called the meeting to order. Everyone rose to recite the Serenity Prayer:

> *God, grant me the serenity to accept the things I cannot change,*
> *The courage to change the things I can,*
> *And the wisdom to know the difference.*

Preliminary announcements were made regarding designated smoking areas, restroom locations in the building, and future meeting locations. There was mention of an upcoming AA/NA banquet (much anticipated according to the respondent ovation), and a request was made for volunteers to clean up after the meeting adjourned. More than two dozen people, including me, raised our hands, offering service.

Finally the guest speaker was introduced. A bearded and balding bear of a man in his sixties approached the microphone-mounted dais to a round of obligatory applause. Then the room fell silent as the bear tested the working condition of both his vocal cords and the sound system by clearing his throat into the mic. Several people chuckled. I winced.

"Hi, my name is Louis and I'm an addict," he began with the customary pretestimony greeting.

"Hi, Louis!" the room responded cheerily.

"It's been twenty-three years since I last used," he announced to thunderous applause, but even as the audience roared their appreciation for Louis's most impressive achievement, a sudden, inexplicable fear came over me—a cold and nameless dread that spiraled up from the small of my back along my spine to impale my brain like an icy harpoon. I couldn't understand it. Something in Louis's words filled me with an oppressive sense of *hopelessness*. At first I thought that with more than two decades of sobriety to boast, the bear was far and away out of my league in terms of recovery time. Twenty-three years, after all, is a long time—almost as long as I'd been alive. I was outclassed, awed, jealous.

No, that wasn't it. It was… something else.

Louis's testimony—much like any other you hear at these meetings—went on to describe his life "lived on life's terms," a life slowly but steadily rebounding from the ravages of the disease of his addiction to painkillers. Having had the misfortune of inheriting a rare form of arthritis that attacked his knees when he was just twenty-two, Louis began to abuse prescription Percocet until DEA restrictions forced him to acquire that and related drugs by any means he could. The addiction lingered ten years after the surgeries that all but eliminated his arthritis, making him just another junkie. Louis talked about the loss of his job and then his fiancée, and the ultimatum imposed by his dad and siblings to get help or be disowned. For Louis the "bottom" came in the form of a mild stroke one day after his thirty-seventh birthday. Louis went almost directly from the hospital to a rehab facility in Newark. Today, the dock manager for an import/export company, Louis thanked his "higher power" for giving him the strength to get clean and stay clean while enjoying restored relationships and regained trust with family and friends. And while the urge to relapse was always there and "dogging" him, Louis said in conclusion, "I take life one day at a time, which, after all, is all any blessed addict can do, am I right?"

With that the room erupted in applause and cheers (Louis was a hit), but above the din I could hear my own heartbeat, a distressed thumping in my ears. The heavyset lady in the seat next to me said something—something meant to gain a reply from me, I think—but I barely heard.

I hadn't been Louis' most attentive listener since he started his testimony. My mind kept winding back to his opening statement as I struggled to determine what it was in those first words that troubled me.

Then it came to me: Louis had not abused drugs in twenty-three years, yet the first thing he did was introduce himself as an addict.

And there was more: his testimony was that of a man who had overcome, yet there was no ring of victory in his words, not a hint of joy about him. Louis didn't speak as someone who had triumphed in a great personal struggle. He sounded like someone too busy staying clean to be happy.

As the applause subsided, I looked around, searching for what I was thinking and feeling on another face—*any* other face. But as I said, Louis was a smash; his story of recovery was apparently a success.

Forgetting I had volunteered to stay and help clean up, I went home in a daze, my mind a dank and dismal fog. I showered and lay in my clean bed in my clean bedroom in that clean-if-slightly-run-down boardinghouse and wrestled with the dread and confusion that refused to let me sleep. I had accumulated three whole months of sobriety. I thought to myself, *If I continue as recovery practices dictate, apply all the steps and principles to my life, if all goes well and I don't screw it up, if I'm lucky, in another thirty-two years and nine months I can be Louis.*

Two weeks later I was sitting in that clean bedroom jabbing a cocaine-loaded syringe into my arm.

Two years after that, I was sentenced to twenty years at Rahway State Prison for armed robbery and atrocious assault. I had at last managed to add the violence to my record that I'd avoided in previous years, giving the state the leverage it needed to hit me with real time. I also had the dubious honor of being the last person in the state of New Jersey to be sentenced for a violent crime legally termed "atrocious." I would walk into that prison at age twenty-nine and then out at forty-one, having served almost twelve of those twenty years. I would not enjoy a single day of my thirties as a free man. Not a single day.

But that night as I lay in my room replaying Louis's appallingly disheartening testimony in my mind and listening for answers to questions I whispered in the dark and getting none … somewhere inside me, something not *of* me smiled.

CHAPTER TWO

Those two years prior to my incarceration at East Jersey State Prison (Rahway) are a vague memory. I remember running—lots of running. I remember graduating from shoplifting and burglary to robbery and still more running. I remember hearing from my brother Michael that Richard had come to Mom's house in search of me when I had stopped reporting to probation. A warrant had been issued for my arrest, and Mike warned me that I should avoid visiting Mom's unless I was looking to get popped. I remember lying to Mike that I'd see Richard and get the matter straightened out, and I remember Mike telling me what he thought I was full of.

I remember sitting in one drug den or another, face sunken, skin ashen, wild-eyed, and pumping cocaine into my system like there was no tomorrow. I remember, each time I withdrew the spent syringe from my arm, that rush of panic as I wondered how I'd acquire the finances for my next hit. And again I remember running.

I don't recall eating much and of course it showed. I won't even venture to guess how much I weighed when the law finally collared me. Before then I slept about as often as I ate. The boarding-house room was long gone, replaced by any abandoned property I could break and enter for a few hours' rest. I remember wearing the same clothes for weeks on end and I remember bathing even less often than I changed.

I remember more running.

And I remember them. Inside me.

Then again, maybe "remember" isn't the right word, since remembering suggests prior knowledge as gained from information or acquaintance—neither of which I ever had. There were no moving images or shapes to perceive, no voices or sounds of any kind to alert me to their existence. I was merely *aware* they were there. That night after the meeting—before my sobriety lay slaughtered on the floor of a shooting gallery on Walnut Avenue—as I lay in the darkness with Louis' depressingly dismal testimony echoing in my head, suddenly and with dark certainty *I just knew.* I was not alone in the room …

I was not alone in *me.*

I don't remember wondering who or what they were; nor do I clearly recall where they came from. I was just overcome with the sensation of their malignant and malevolent *presence.* They were real and alive and...*inside me.*

I remember suddenly feeling terrified and then just as suddenly dismissing it all as imagination. I attended two more meetings the next week, hearing not so much as a word spoken at either, and then shooting cocaine the week after. As my condition deteriorated, I remember the smug, self-righteous looks I got from neighbors and other acquaintances who had predicted my relapse.

That was when the running started. It stopped one morning in October when I ran into my mother near downtown. She was on her way to pay the house utility bills and asked—no, begged me to walk with her. She insisted that I needed help, a more comprehensive recovery program than that twenty-one-day "spa" I'd completed. Of course I wasn't listening; I could barely even look at her. I needed a hit. My mind raced to contrive a possible income source. I'll never forget the look of despair on that woman's face as she gave up and went her way, or the shame that knifed through me as I watched my mother, heartbroken and morose, head downtown.

Only hours later I was sitting in the Trenton lockup, charged with the assault of a convenience store employee in the course of a robbery. To this day the details of the incident remain sketchy as I was a little desperate and more than a little frightened at the time but apparently I had cut the guy. They say I nearly killed him.

Then—for the next eleven years, anyway—the running stopped.

CHAPTER THREE

"I'm gonna miss you, Mitch," Danny said for the third time since the session began. "Far as I'm concerned, you 'bout the only one in this whole business that keeps it real." Almost all the other men in attendance nodded or muttered something in agreement.

The "whole business" as Danny referred to it went by the more popular name, New Directions, a drug-abuse rehabilitation program founded by the inmates at Rahway. Funded entirely out of our own pockets: every textbook and training manual, letterhead stationery, office supplies, every piece of information published on the subject of addiction education from chemical dependency to relapse prevention was paid for by us, the offenders, the criminals, the recovering addicts. We, the inmate staff of New Directions had even composed our own recovery format, a tri-phased, peer-treatment process as thorough and comprehensive as that of any civilian state-run facility. Although we had little or no formal education in the field of psychology or any of the related behavioral sciences, we had the not-inconsiderable advantage of an intimate knowledge of drug culture.

It also benefited us that the world outside Rahway knew about us. We'd been the focus of many newscasts, both local and national, gaining positive coverage in their human interest stories. More importantly, the prison administration respected us to the point where we were given our own office and the three classrooms in which we conducted encounter or therapy groups and instruction sessions. We've had visits from celebrities like Ben Vereen and Jim Brown, who introduced his Amer-I-can program at the prison. New Directions was a source of immense pride for its founders, men determined to break the endless cycle of addiction, crime, and incarceration. They were men undeniably dedicated to recovery education; they taught and counseled with an unquenchable passion. A few had pursued an advanced education via correspondence courses, but hardcore experience more than college degrees qualified them as true professionals.

While I was not present at its inception, New Directions was only a few years old when I arrived at Rahway in 1986. I didn't get involved with the program until 1989. My first few years at the prison were, to say the least, tough. For a long time I subsisted on denial. I couldn't wrap my mind around the twenty-year sentence I'd received. I filed one groundless appeal after another; all were denied. Then—just a little desperate, I confess—I resorted to begging, sending letters to the governor requesting clemency on the grounds that my violent crime was the product of a drug-addled mind; had I been free of the disease of addiction, I'd have never committed such an appallingly heinous act. A valid plea, I thought—the governor didn't agree.

I was a little less than two years into my incarceration when the curtain of my denial was raised and the reality of my situation began to dawn on me. Bitterness and resentment blended inside me, manifesting in rebellious and self-destructive behavior. I became uncooperative, hostile, and belligerent; railing against a system I had no hope of defeating. On numerous occasions I was warned by corrections officers that they had something special in the oven for "tough guys" like me. My routine response was to challenge them to bring it on, and they were more than happy to oblige, dragging me off to Administrative Segregation (Ad Seg), the knobby tip of a riot club pressed firmly against the base of my spine to coax me along. Almost always my arrival at my 8' × 10' cell in Ad Seg would culminate in a spirited reception involving the guards' gloved fists against my not-so-protected torso. When it came to demonstrating their sovereignty over the prison population, the COs did a splendid job. Unfortunately I was not as good a learner as they were teachers; I cursed them during the beat downs and spat obscenities after them when they left me bruised and aching in my cell. Sometimes my taunts brought them back for seconds, but usually they just moved on, leaving me to vent my rage into the dark and close confines of solitary.

The last time it happened I stood at the center of my cell, my head throbbing as though it would explode. It was the worst headache I ever had, probably the result of my screaming threats and insults since my beating had not included blows to the head (they were careful about that). Rubbing my temples with the index and middle fingers of both hands, I pressed my back against the cold concrete wall and sank to the even colder concrete floor. As my weight shifted from my feet to my seat, I became aware of a dull throb in my right ankle. I didn't remember hurting it. I remember only the anger boiling inside me like the interior of an active volcano. I thought, *if I could lay my hands on just one of those uniformed punks, I'd…*

I'd *what?* I'm a prisoner, an inmate sentenced to dwell in their world for the next two decades. This was their jurisdiction, their domain. I had no authority, no power here. I had nothing.

What in the world did I think I could do to them?

Every now and then—when the circumstances didn't sufficiently torment me—I'd finish the job myself by looking back at my life and wondering: *What happened to me? How did I come to this?* I'd send my memory as far back as it would go, trying to find that turn in the road I shouldn't have taken, where reason slipped away and insanity moved in. Hazy memories of harmless youthful indulgences would answer my search, revealing nothing so broken, no character flaw so vile as to warrant such an outcome as this. I looked for the incident, the event that took a fairly normal and reasonably intelligent young man and placed his feet on a path leading to drug abuse, crime, and prison. Again I found no satisfactory answer, so I abandoned the search. One's past is a useless concept to ponder, full of second-guessing and regret: *What if I'd done this instead of that?* and *If only I'd gone here and not there.* The past is good for nothing.

Beaten, morose, and alone, I laid my bald head against the wall of my cell and asked, "What now?" into the still, musty air.

As if in reply, someone laughed beyond the brief space comprising my lockdown, a crazy, mocking shriek that trailed along the walls and hung in the air around me. It seemed to close in on all sides like it was trying to crush me—or draw me in.

I couldn't breathe. A mind-numbing fear shuddered through me. I drew my knees up to my chest and closed my eyes.

For the first time since my incarceration, I contemplated the possibility of actually dying in this place.

Then—in the darkness, with my fear and loneliness and with the thought of death an oppressive black cloud in my mind... *they* came.

No, that's not right. To say they came implies they had arrived from somewhere else, that they were not there all along—and I know they were.

They *appeared*—but that's not quite right either. I didn't see them—not exactly. They lurked and huddled inside me, creatures of shadowy substance and form with pupil-less slits for eyes. I couldn't see them—I just know that's how they looked.

I couldn't see them, but I could feel them, feel their malevolent presence, feel their evil intent. They didn't move or speak. They only watched. Watched me with lethal black loathing.

They were there—but there *where?* In my mind, nestled in my subconscious like a repressed childhood memory of unbearable abuse? Or perhaps they'd taken up residency in my gut. Sometimes in the midst of some of the worst things I'd done to get high, my belly would flip, as if something in there was reacting to the enormity of my behavior. Asian cultures believe that the belly is a person's spiritual center, that his spirit resides there. That's why Buddha's is so big.

I trembled, the fear holding me, refusing to let me go. *What are they?* I wondered. *What do they want with me?*

Then the answer came, rolling in on the memory of meetings and counseling and sharing from my days at the Pit Stop.

They're my addiction... they're my disease in spirit form, come to gloat over what they'd done to me, come to laugh over this mess they made of my life.

I opened my eyes (they'd grown accustomed to my lightless surroundings by now) and surveyed my cell: a box unfit for the storage of a living person. A crypt.

And I decided I would not die here—not in this cell and not in this prison.

I decided to accept the consequences of my actions and surrender to my circumstances. I would lose the "tough guy" attitude. I would stop fighting my losing battle with the system and comply, go along, get along.

I thought, *I'm going to do my time and get out of here. I will not*

*end up just another junkie loser swallowed up by my disease. I'll
beat this thing. Whatever it took. Whatever I had to do.*

I'll beat this thing.

One week after my release from Ad Seg, I signed up for the
GED program. The administration—or at least that segment of it
that dealt most directly with me—was understandably surprised
and more than a little dubious about my turnaround. Almost
from the very start of my incarceration I had earned a reputation
as a "hard case," one who simply will not cooperate readily,
comply immediately, or go quietly. For a time the COs regarded
me warily, suspecting my change of heart as a ploy, a mask for
ulterior motives of God knows what nature. Whatever diverse and
fantastic speculations they entertained among themselves when
they discussed me, they no doubt unanimously agreed that sooner
or later my cursing, spitting, angry real self would show once
again. Therefore, they were probably surprised again when the two
instructors who prepared their classes for the General Equivalency
Exam submitted reports that said I was a good student, that I was
smart and learned well. As time for the exams rolled around, the
words "strong candidate" were often used in the same sentence
with my name. I soaked in the praise and actually studied harder,
improving my math (my toughest subject) skills.

I signed up for the New Directions recovery course the same
week I took the exams. Nine months later I had both a GED and a
certificate of completion from the inmate-run program added to
my prison file. Most of the founding members had been released on
parole or transferred to reduced-security facilities by then, but Eric,
the New Directions chairman, was still there. More than halfway
through a twenty-five-year bid for a drug-related homicide and
due for his first appearance before the parole board soon, Eric had
made New Directions his passion. During his imprisonment, Eric
had received several college-course degrees including a master's

in sociology, plus his Certified Drug and Alcohol Counselor's certificate. Eric either composed or helped compose the format for all three phases: Confession and Surrender, which focused on the individual learning to abandon his denial and face the truth of his addiction; Social Dysfunction and Healing, which dealt with the impact of the addict's disease upon the lives of others, at home, in the workplace and elsewhere; and New Horizons, where a man began to envision, discuss, and plan a life free of substances. Eric monitored the facilitation of each group, appointing or replacing leaders by recruiting former clients he believed to be earnestly pursuing recovery. Two weeks before I was due to complete the third and final phase, Eric asked me if I would stay on and replace Barkley as Social Dysfunction and Healing facilitator. Barkley, nearing the end of a five-year bid for manslaughter, had already appeared before the parole board and his release date was just weeks away. Honored by Eric's invitation and now quite passionate about New Directions myself, I not only accepted, but with Eric's consent brought updated material to the class.

I was a different person from the hostile, burnt-out druggie that entered Rahway three years prior. Recovery programs such as New Directions, the Pit Stop, and a rehab I went to even before that (more on that later) place a strong emphasis on the disease of addiction being a permanent condition, a never-ending battle with "triggers": people, places, and things. We who had been unfortunate enough to fall into the trap of addiction were addicts for life, but addiction didn't have to have the last word in our lives. By accepting our powerlessness over our disease and with the help of our "higher power," we could live full and complete, drug-free lives. Like someone living with HIV or hepatitis C, we had a disease, but the disease didn't have to have us.

As time rolled by, it became evident even to the most skeptical observer that I was a changed man, serious about my recovery and equally serious about helping others achieve theirs. People—inmates and administration alike—started to respect me; I liked that. I didn't just throw myself into my role as a New Directions facilitator but lived and practiced the principles we preached. By 1994 I had been a prison inmate at Rahway for nine years, more than five as a positive role model for recovery. I avoided the underground activity at the prison and conducted myself with honesty and integrity—qualities that apparently distinguished me from some of the program's other staff members.

One of Eric's last acts as chairman before making parole in the spring of 1994 was to have me promoted to the position of clinical director, which was a fancy title for secretary, really. I still headed the phase II group meeting but now had the added chore of composing daily membership rosters for prison records, answering applications for admission to classes submitted by inmates with upcoming parole hearings (it seemed a certificate of completion from New Directions was an achievement of some influence with the parole board), and making phone calls inviting various addiction specialists and the odd celebrity to guest speak at our annual banquets.

I lost myself in the business of recovery, becoming better acquainted with the clients than with the staff. I barely knew the other facilitators or Doug, who was the chairman at the time. Outside staff meetings and office hours I rarely saw any of them. Many of the clients, however, knew one or two of them only too well, and I didn't like the reports they brought concerning my colleagues.

"Man, when you leave, this machine ain't gonna be worth the paper they print your graduation on," Danny complained, "and that ain't no lie."

Danny was only a few years younger than I and had confessed to being involved with the penal system most of his life. He often boasted of having served time (or "a tour of duty," as he called it) at every prison in New Jersey except Trenton State. A little cocky and more than a little guarded when he started New Directions, Danny had come a long way. Once hostile and sarcastic in his group participation, Danny had come to lend valuable input, seeking answers for himself as well as for others. He reminded me of my days at the Pit Stop, as he discovered in himself an honest desire to find a life beyond his addiction, beyond crime and incarceration. More than once he attributed his change of heart in no small part to the example I presented. Others had said the same, an honor I tried to accept with humility.

"It ain't as bad as all that, Danny," I told him, but the words sounded weak even as I said them. I had heard that Salim, the phase I facilitator, was "dipping and dabbing," indulging in recreational drug use. It had come by more than one source that he was having heroin smuggled in to him during monthly visits from his girl. There were also mumblings that Butler, the New Horizons leader, sold as well as smoked marijuana and was not terribly restrictive regarding those with whom he did business—even clients! Artis, the New Directions treasurer, had been accused of going into program funds for personal reasons. Worst of all, Doug seemed oblivious not only to wrongdoing by staff members but to the complaints of the membership, which in and of itself made Doug the object of suspicious speculation.

I grew uncomfortable, embarrassed under the gaze of my group. I didn't know how to respond to Danny's concerns. The truth was there was no way to hold a New Directions staff member accountable for his actions—at least not on a peer level. Founded and run by the inmates, New Directions was self-supporting and self-sufficient. The prison administration held no interest in the ethical conduct of program staff except as it applied to prison rules. They would quickly prosecute drug use or larceny as it came to their attention, and if the program proved itself a corrupt or crooked enterprise, they would just as quickly shut us down. Apart from someone going to the administrator's office with evidence of criminal activity, which would never happen, we were on our own, left to deal with in-house discord by ourselves. We had neither the might nor the means to police ourselves; each man operated in his post according to his conscience. I thought about the New Directions I joined half a decade ago, and my heart grew heavy with grief.

"Danny, I don't mean to put down what you're sayin', but you gotta keep your focus on what you're here for." A twinge of guilt came with the words. I'd used that statement for its therapeutic application, to redirect a client who'd become distracted or tempted by the many circumstances prison can present. Now it felt like an evasion. More and more my group sessions were becoming forums for gripes by the membership against the staff, with me on point, avoiding the issues, indirectly defending the culprits. Chagrined, I thought I was getting pretty adept at blowing smoke. "What the next man's doing ain't got nothin' to do with what you need to be doing. Besides, not all the brothers with the program are as messed up as you seem to think." This was true enough, but being put on the defensive about an organization I once held in high regard made me feel ashamed and angry.

Walter joined in. "Yeah, Mitch, we know all that, but I gotta tell you, bro, I been seein' some sorry stuff goin' down with some of your boys. I mean, suspect stuff, you dig?"

I nodded, buying myself time to think. Five years ago I could not have imagined myself in a position of being the good one, the one people liked. It was an image that meant a lot to me, one I was not about to risk now by invalidating the mood of the group with therapeutic double talk. "Look, guys, I hear everything you're sayin'. I hear the talk about what's goin' on and you're right: it's sorry. But when you get right down to it, it all comes back to what're you gonna do? I mean, look at us: a bunch of hardcore dope fiends tryin' to get our lives back before we lose them, before this disease kills us or puts us in one of these places for good. We've seen and done stuff that'll be with us forever, things we'd take back in a heartbeat if we could. And for what? To keep pumpin' that poison in our bodies; killin' ourselves on the installment plan." I waited, letting the rest of it come slowly, trying to sound more genuine than textbook, and wary that I'd given this speech to this group before. "And now here we are in this prison and in this program. One day we're gonna get out. We'll be free again, and if we're lucky we'll never see the inside of one of these places again. But right now we got a chance to learn about this disease before it messes us up even more than it's already done. That means learnin' from the good *and* the bad. If nothin' else, let the bad ones remind you of what you don't wanna be no more, the life you're tryin' to leave behind."

Stanley weighed in. "Yeah, but they *ain't* behind us; they're in our *face*—in our face with that *stuff*!" At twenty-two, Stanley was the youngest member of the group, only into his second year of a ten-year sentence for carjacking and assault. "Next month I start the New Horizons class and I gotta tell you, man, I ain't feelin' it. I know the dude who's runnin' the class and I *know* what he's doin'. Weed was my thing, Mitch. How'm I s'posed to get better when the teacher's somebody I can cop from? What am I s'posed to learn from somebody like that?" Commiserate mumbling among the group rewarded the statement.

"He ain't the teacher, Stanley," I said, "just the facilitator." I flushed as an assortment of jeers answered my correction. "Listen, I'm just sayin' that all we bring to the table is technical stuff: information, printed materials, films, stuff like that. We organize meetings and take attendance and issue certificates, but you guys bring the education. Any real learnin' that comes out of these groups comes from *you*. When it comes down to it, what can I teach you about addiction that you don't already know from bein' out there? I learn more listenin' to you brothers than you could ever learn from me. It's about sharin' your experiences, comparin' your lives and getting' to the feelings you had when you were goin' through the things you went through. That's where your recovery comes from—not from some guy takin' attendance and handin' out papers, but from *you*. That's the kind of strong foundation a drug-free life is built on, a life nobody can stop you from gettin' no matter what they may or may not be doin'." For a moment the mood of the room seemed pacified as the men considered all I'd said. But it was an uneasy calm, resting more on their regard for me than for my rhetoric. After a moment Danny broke the cumbersome silence.

"That's all well and good, Mitch, but tell me somethin': if you really mean all that, then how come you're quittin'?"

CHAPTER FOUR

The problem as I saw it was that New Directions didn't conduct peer review or accountability meetings for the staff personnel. We had no forum at which we could confront one another regarding conduct or behavior. I knew the others only on a superficial level. I'd see them in the yard, in the cafeteria at mealtimes, or in the dome-ceilinged auditorium on movie night. We were from different parts of the state and so were not at all acquainted before coming to Rahway. Men from Trenton tended to associate with other men from Trenton; likewise Newark and so on. Salim, a native of Camden, facilitated the phase I (*Confession and Surrender*) group. I didn't like Salim. Seven years my junior, he was ignorant, obnoxious, and immature. Unable to fully comprehend the format written for the group he chaired, Salim often deviated from it altogether, turning the meetings into open discussion sessions and presiding over them as if he had all the answers. He was quick to interject his ideas, however irrelevant, on a shared testimony as though he believed the position of facilitator meant solving everyone's problems. His input—inaccurately gleaned from some book or stolen from someone of true wisdom—he offered as the hard-learned lessons of his own life.

But the men in his group knew Salim was full of it. Rumors of his monthly "visits" with his girlfriend were so casually bantered about, I was surprised that some CO hadn't overheard. I can speak neither to the truth nor the falsehood of the accusations; I knew only that because of guys like Salim, enrolling in the New Directions program had become little more than a necessary evil: men doing time for drug-related offenses needed the certificate of completion to prove to the parole board that they were availing themselves of every opportunity for self-rehabilitation the prison offered. Outside that piece of paper, most who enrolled didn't believe New Directions had anything to offer; it was just another racket. When men like Rodney and Paul and Eric were at the helm, New Directions was a force for good. Their integrity and passion for addiction education and recovery encouraged and inspired me. I wanted to be like them, to have the confidence in my recovery that they had in theirs. I wanted the strength to seize my addiction by the collar and let it know that I was in charge; it could no longer enslave and control me. And then I wanted to share that strength with others. Those men made New Directions larger than life. It seemed a great deal smaller now.

We met on a Thursday night in March 1995. Ostensibly we were there to plan the program's banquet for that summer, but my instincts alerted me to a confrontational feel in the room. Had I known an ambush was in the works, I'd have worn a vest—or at least a cup.

"So what's all this noise about you all up in my business?" And just like that it was on. The tone was ignorant and hostile—characteristically Salim. I looked over from the desk where I sat; unsure at whom the question had been directed. Salim was standing beside Doug near the chalk board and glaring in my direction. I supposed, therefore, he was talking to me.

"What?"

"I didn't stutter, did I?" Salim responded in exactly the manner

I would expect from a punk like him. "I said, what's this about you askin' people if I'm usin'?"

That wasn't precisely the truth. After parrying accusations about Salim *ad nauseum*, I made the mistake of asking Doug if he too had heard the rumors. I had grown weary of apologizing for the character of my colleagues and so had gone to the chairman, hoping, I guess, for an ally in confronting negative attitudes and unethical behavior in our organization. I'd been a fool. Doug had said we would discuss the matter at this meeting. Nothing in his demeanor indicated this is what he meant.

I should have known. Salim had ingratiated himself to Doug and had been his yes-man for at least as long as they'd held their respective posts with the program. Now it seems Doug had told Salim I'd been talking about him. I looked at the two of them standing together and felt embarrassed and angry with myself for having been so stupid.

"All I did was ask Doug if he heard anything about you usin'," I said evenly.

"So how come you askin' questions 'bout what I'm doin'?" Even with Doug beside him, it took a supreme effort on Salim's part to maintain eye contact with me. For everything else I disliked about Salim, I also found him cowardly—the type who found his courage in the crowd. I doubt he ever did anything—legal or otherwise—that required him to stand alone. Of course that wouldn't be an issue tonight since obviously Doug had his back. "You got somethin' you wanna ask me, I'm right here."

I laced my fingers on my desktop and took a breath, my embarrassment ebbing away; the anger remained, though now not so self-directed. "Okay, Salim—*are* you usin'?"

But evidently asking Salim to his face didn't warrant any more respect than asking others behind his back. I half-suspected he didn't believe I'd ask even though he challenged me to do so. "Hey, man, who're you to be askin' me if I'm usin'? I don't remember nobody makin' you chairman of New Directions. What happened, did you have your own election and vote yourself in charge and forget to tell the rest of us?" A few others in attendance found this funny, though I thought their respondent chuckles were forced. Case, the New Directions secretary, was a friend of Salim's mainly because they were roughly the same age and were housed in the same trailer unit in the industrial area of the prison. Case's laugh, usually a loud and annoying cackle, like that of some oversized scavenger bird, was less so, given that Salim might be trying to steer this discussion into deep, possibly violent waters. Still, his laugh—even subdued—ground on my nerves like sandpaper. Butler—the other name I was constantly hearing in connection to drug use—also laughed.

And then there was O'Brian, membership coordinator, the newest staff member and the only white. O'Brian, no doubt hoping to be omitted from the matter, didn't laugh. I had spoken with O'Brian on many occasions since he joined New Directions. He was almost always in the office when I arrived to compose the dailies. His job was to assign new members to the orientation class headed by Doug and then compose the attendees' list for the group cycles. Once he confided to me that he wanted to be a certified drug counselor. I liked O'Brian but didn't expect I'd get much support from him tonight—not that I blamed him. I turned my attention back to Salim.

"No, Salim, I ain't in charge. I'm just tired of hearin' your name in every group, sick and tired of people askin' me where you get the nerve to run a recovery class when you ain't even in recovery."

That got exactly the rise out of Salim that I expected—and wanted. He recoiled as if struck, and then he arched his back, trying to appear taller and more menacing than his stature naturally presented. "What people? Who's sayin' that about me?"

I shook my head, unmoved by Salim's feigned indignation. Doug then joined the exchange with his feigned objectivity. "Now, that ain't really fair, is it, Mitch? I mean, if somebody's spreadin' rumors that serious about the brother, he's got a right to know who it is, don't he? Because that kinda talk can land a man in the hole, know what I mean?"

I nodded, pretending to think about it. Part of me wanted to tell him, reveal the names of the many guys who had come to me regarding Salim's underground activities. Most of them detested Salim and would love to have him confront them about what they'd told me—not that I believed he'd have the guts to do so even with Doug at his back. This was all smoke, a dodge to keep me on the defensive and the focus off Salim.

"I ain't givin' up no names," I finally replied.

Salim—as I knew he would—took great delight in this. "Prob'ly 'cause ain't no names to give. Prob'ly 'cause the only one tellin' these lies 'bout me is you." He stood glaring at me, a self-satisfied smirk curling his pink lips. I locked my gaze into his and in an instant conveyed every hateful, homicidal impulse I ever felt in one white-hot leer. And for a gratifying instant it seemed to get through. Salim blinked, looked away, and then with effort reset himself. I forced myself not to smile in victory.

"Do you care to respond?" Doug asked in program-speak: a challenge to a client who had been confronted by one or more of his peers for his negative behavior or for an offense he'd committed against another client. First the offender is "put on point," made to sit and listen quietly while his peers "grouped him" or voiced their complaints or criticisms. Then he is asked if he would "care to respond" or answer only to the concerns raised in humble and contrite fashion. I had been put on point, I had been grouped, and now I was expected to answer in humble and contrite fashion.

I looked at Doug, embarrassed again and furious. I didn't honestly believe I could take Doug one-on-one. He was bigger, stronger, and had led a more violent life than I. I always suspected the primary reason he'd been appointed New Directions chairman was because he was an imposing, commanding presence—attributes that were undeniable assets when it came to dealing with prison inmates. In any case, *mano a mano* with Doug, whatever my chances, wouldn't happen as long as a gutless wonder like Salim was present to join the fray. Defeated and humiliated, I shook my head again. "No. I don't wanna respond."

For the first time since this ambush was launched, Doug moved away from Salim, positioning himself more toward front-and-center in the classroom. "In that case, how 'bout we close this matter and get to the business we came here for: plannin' this year's banquet." At that the room itself seemed to breathe a sigh of relief. The mood lightened, several comments—unintelligible to me—were made. I just sat, feeling like I'd been blindfolded, my hands cuffed behind my back, and beaten. Seeing my discomfiture, Doug stepped in again in all his sovereign chairmanship. "Look, man, we need to put this behind us and work together. How we gonna be able to keep the clients in line if they see we don't have each other's back?"

Keep the clients in line, I thought. *Since when is that what we're about?*

"We got to support each other," Doug continued and I could see the others had returned their attention to me, nodding or commenting in support of Doug's remarks. "We have to make it known that if somebody has somethin' negative to say about any staff member, he better be ready to back it up or shut it up. I can respect you for not givin' up any names, Mitch, and I don't think those accusations came from you. But if somebody's gonna put out news that serious about one of us, he ought to be man enough to take responsibility for it."

Another reason Doug was effective in the leadership role: his ability to promote solidarity among the troops. He had managed to inject an "us versus them" attitude into the minds of the staff—and they ate it up. Even the neutral O'Brian was quick to join his wagon to the circle. The question of Salim getting high even as he facilitated a recovery group meeting was no longer an issue. What mattered now was that apparently the clients of New Directions were out to malign and discredit the staff, and I had been branded their collaborator. I shrank inside myself, feeling sick.

"How 'bout you brothers shake hands and peace it out," Butler suggested with an enthusiasm that poured over me like ice water, "and let's plan this banquet."

Doug would never have made such an abysmally stupid suggestion. He made no effort to support Butler for making it, and Salim and I did not "peace it out."

That summer for the first time since I joined New Directions, I did not go to the annual banquet.

I never sat in on another phase II meeting either.

Several weeks prior to that night I had submitted my more or less formal notice of resignation from the New Directions program. As I explained to Doug, I'd been a staff member since I completed the process as a client almost five years ago, longer than any of the current members, including Doug, had been on staff. I was feeling a little burnt out, I told Doug, and with my time in prison winding down, I needed more time to myself, time to make outside connections for employment and housing, time to prepare myself to appear before the parole board. I would stay with my present group until the end of their twelve-week cycle. He would have to find a new facilitator for the next group, not to mention a new secretary—that is, a clinical director. That's much the way I told it to my group the night Danny asked why I was quitting. I thought it was a plausible enough explanation, preferable to confessing my dislike for the hypocrites who were my colleagues and my distaste for the dishonor they'd brought to a program I once held in stellar regard.

Anyway, plausible or not, Danny and the group didn't buy it, and my "colleagues" didn't care. Neither did I anymore.

So after that staff meeting, I quit showing up. I never went back to the office, never submitted another roster, never mailed another letter or placed another phone call. I didn't even keep my word to finish the last four weeks with my group.

I just quit.

CHAPTER FIVE

The truth was I was no better than any of them: Salim, Butler, or Doug. Despite the sterling example of rehabilitation and recovery I'd presented and for all my righteous indignation for the others' hypocrisy, I was the same as they, perhaps worse, since as it turned out I was selling a product that—in the deepest part of me—I found appalling and unacceptable.

It wasn't that I was not sincere. It wasn't that I didn't try. I must have read every report, article, and technical journal (including thirty-eight volumes of the *Diagnostic and Statistical Manual of Mental Disorders)* ever printed on the subject of addiction. I'd watched the televised discussions featuring medical experts and addiction specialists, and I'd studied the formats of many of the more renowned rehab facilities. I myself had upgraded the phase II format to include the newly published therapeutic techniques of well-known clinical psychologists. Like Eric and Barkley and the others before the likes of Doug and his ilk, I was on fire for recovery; passionately and tirelessly immersed in therapeutic concepts and treatment modalities. There had been a time when I was considering pursuing a degree in counseling. I was as thoroughly about the business of recovery as any one person could be.

But even in the best of times I wrestled with the idea that I was stricken with a disease for which there was only treatment and no cure. I was never able to fully come to terms with the notion of spending the rest of my life keeping this insidious malady I had in remission. I taught it, discussed it, and preached it objectively and convincingly. I just couldn't accept it, couldn't accept that because of my bad decisions I was forever diminished, that something fine had been removed from me and something detestable added.

Something fine removed—what would that something fine be? *Innocence,* maybe, or something as similar to it as anyone beyond the age of adolescence may claim. After all, I had experienced, seen, and done things that had changed me for all time and not for the better. I had learned things I wish I could unlearn, knew things I felt damned for knowing. In the years to come, when I thought of Salim and the others, I'd wonder if my resentment of them was grounded in the grim truth they knew and that I did not: that recovery is a fool's errand, a process of limited achievement and even more limited satisfaction, and that rehab is a crock. Maybe— unlike me—the others had come to terms with the cold finality of their condition and were simply making use of New Directions for all it could really offer: accolades and occupation. To expect or even want anything more was a foolish waste of time.

Because when it was all over, when the last testimony was shared, the last pamphlet read, when the last meeting was adjourned, we were still addicts, abusers, junkies, dope fiends, crack heads, meth freaks, and drunks. We are the diseased; in the struggle of our lives for the rest of our lives to get one more day clean. If my former colleagues, the new guard of New Directions had considered the folly of combating the incurable with a genuine expectation of victory, then maybe they weren't being hypocritical, just pragmatic.

But I did not consider it—not for the remainder of my time at Rahway. I hated the men who had muddied the good name of

New Directions, and I found new interests, like weight lifting and pen-pal dating. I also remained drug free, remained positive in my recovery, and remained on the right side of prison rules and regulations.

In March 1996, Doug was convicted of murder and sentenced to life without possibility of parole at Trenton State Prison just four months after his parole from Rahway.

In February 1997, Eric, my friend and New Directions mentor, was killed in a drug deal gone wrong with a Columbian gang in New York. Reports say Eric was tortured with knives for many hours before he finally died.

In September 1997, after more than eleven years of incarceration I was paroled from East Jersey State Prison. I walked out of that institution with a GED, nearly a dozen certificates for my involvement with New Directions as a client and then staff member, my official New Directions jacket (a red nylon windbreaker with *MITCH: Clin. Dir.* in gold silk thread on the left breast), a healthier, fairly muscular physique, and $700 I'd saved working in the furniture upholstery and repair shop.

I also had a head full of therapeutic concept, full knowledge of the twelve steps and twelve traditions of both AA and NA, and eleven years of clean and sober time.

And I had a plan: to find a job and a place to live, to find a wife, and to create a new life, never to see the inside of another prison. First and foremost I had the unshakable commitment to be clean and sober forever, attend meetings, find a sponsor, work the steps, and face life on life's terms.

With all that I walked out of Rahway prison and returned to freedom, returned to the world.

And the gods of addiction returned with me.

CHAPTER SIX

I went to live at my mother's for a time. Her door was always open to me when I was clean (and often even when I wasn't, but I'll get to that later). Mom had come to visit me as often as she could at Rahway. I know the twenty-year sentence I received had been stressful for her as well as the rest of my nine younger siblings. I know there were times—especially at the start—when she wondered if I'd make it; if I'd leave that place alive or if she'd live to see it. It had crossed my mind, too. I'd spent many a sleepless night recalling that last day: my mother morose and forlorn, walking away after I rejected her, and me under arrest and facing decades of jail time only hours later. In the stillness of my cell I would lie awake and worry, wondering if that would be my last significant memory of us together. Would I ever have another opportunity to make up that last day to her—make up my wasted life to her—and present her with a son who was not lost to drug addiction.

It was good to be at Mom's. For the first six months after I was released, I was required to wear an electronic monitoring anklet and report to Mercer County Parole twice a month for drug testing. By now I had not only been drug free eleven years but hadn't even smoked a cigarette in four. I looked good, younger than my forty-one years. Prison, it seems, has a way of preserving a person even while it's robbing him of years of his life.

I found a job with a furniture company within the first two weeks of my release. I attended AA and NA no less than three nights a week. One night during introductions, I stood and announced that I was fresh out of the joint and in the market for a sponsor. Willie, an ex-con himself, stepped right up to take me on as his sponsee. I was pulling out all the stops, leaving no stone unturned. To Mom's mounting joy I even started going to church, where, as it turned out, I was considered quite the eligible bachelor among some of the women members. After having spent more than a decade in stasis, as it were, I was actually said to be a "catch." I'd never known such popularity before; I was never the sort of man women considered handsome, and I played this new, leading-man role for all it was worth, dating several of the church's romance-minded sisters in leisurely succession.

One night while visiting my brother Val and his wife, Patricia, I met Debra, the divorced mother of two teen boys. A little over a year later we were married. I moved into her house in Levittown, Pennsylvania, while I continued to work at the furniture company in New Jersey, where—to no one's surprise—I was soon promoted to floor supervisor. I also continued to go to church, attend meetings, and maintain my sobriety. I carried myself with confidence and self-assurance; I had life by the horns and my addiction by the throat. I was living proof that I didn't have to be sick just because I had a disease. I was in control, captain of my life.

Time, however—less than two years of it—would prove that I was in control of nothing, and captain of less than nothing.

Often—while in the middle of wherever I was and in the midst of whatever I was doing—I would stop and replay Louis' testimony in my head. More than fourteen years had elapsed since that night, and I can remember with haunting clarity the absence of joy, the lack of victory Louis had to show for more than two decades of sobriety. All these years later his "achievement" still rang hollowly in my memory, echoing in some dark, empty place inside me ...

That dark, empty place where the gods dwelled.

When I left Rahway I knew the twelve steps backward and forward, and I practiced them one *step* at a time. I knew to be wary and identify the *people, places, and things* that threaten recovery and trigger relapse. I knew enough about therapeutic concepts and treatment modalities to facilitate a group discussion or counsel an individual as professionally as the most accredited specialist.

And it would all come to nothing as—just as it happened in Rahway—I would stand alone and condemned for what I *didn't* know.

Several months before Debra and I were to celebrate our second anniversary, I was divorced, unemployed, homeless, and chasing my next fix through the streets of Trenton, the veneer of my recovery stripped away and my façade of therapeutic wisdom penetrated to expose me for the self-deluded fraud I was.

My recovery had been a lie. I had undergone a therapeutic process that had only succeeded in making a cleaner, more attractive host for the gods to occupy, a healthier body for them to degrade, a smarter, more informed mind for them to drive insane.

A better man to destroy. And they were laughing.

They—the gods of addiction—were inside me.

And laughing.

CHAPTER SEVEN

Keep it on the "I": an expression used primarily in recovery group meetings or therapy sessions admonishing a speaker for discussing his experiences or feelings in general terms, such as, "When *we* were doing this," or "when *we* felt like that." It's a good rule, intended to prevent the person sharing from justifying his negative attitudes or escaping responsibility for his misdeeds by losing himself in the crowd, so to speak.

Keep it on the "I." Don't seek out allies in the room. No matter how universal your feelings or common your behavior; irrespective of how many others can relate to your situation. Speak only for yourself. Keep it on the "I."

So ...

It wasn't so much that *I* was opposed to the notion of addiction as a disease. When *I'd* remember the things *I* did: the crimes *I'd* committed, the harm *I'd* brought upon others, the worry and shame *I'd* caused my family and friends; when *I* thought of the depths to which *I'd* sunk, the time *I'd* wasted and the opportunities *I'd* squandered; when *I* thought of the things *I'd* done that can never be undone, my soul cringes with self-revulsion and shame and my spirit cries out for a rationale, a soul-absolving explanation for such unconscionable behavior. For the sake of being able to stand myself

I need a conscience-clearing excuse; a villain upon whom to pin the blame—like the devil or...mental illness.

Yes, there is a measure of comfort that comes with believing it was all symptomatic, that I was sick. It wasn't me; it was the disease. The alternative is that I'm evil—who would prefer that? Sick people receive sympathy; evil people are disdained. Disease garners study, funding, and support; moral turpitude reaps scorn, prosecution, and incarceration.

In the beginning there was a sense of relief that came with believing I had this disease. It became the repository of all the malfunction and dysfunction in my life. The disease made me a liar, a cheat, a thief. It was the disease's fault that I couldn't be believed or trusted; it made me do things that I couldn't bear to remember, let alone confess.

No, I wasn't terribly opposed to the idea that addiction is a disease; I just didn't like having to accept the "disease" as incurable. While I struggled and suffered with the immorality of what my life had become and took minor solace that it was a life corrupted by sickness, I knew in my heart that I didn't want to stay sick. I wanted to get well, to be cured.

Conventional wisdom in recovery circles holds that a full, satisfying, drug-free life is possible in spite of the disease—in other words, being an addict doesn't mean I have to use. But isn't it the nature of a disease in remission to inevitably come out of remission, reinfect, and kill its host? Looking back I think there must have been a part of me that believed so, even as I studied and counseled and abstained and recovered.

I believe that in the deepest part of me I came to accept the concept of recovery as an exercise in futility. Eventually, inevitably, despite all I've learned and no matter how many years, decades, centuries I remained clean and sober, I would succumb to the disease.

Hello, my name is Mitch and I'm an addict. I've been drug-and-alcohol-free for 150 years last Tuesday. Haven't taken so much as an aspirin or smoked a cigarette for a century-and-a-half and still I'm an addict. You see, I have this disease called addiction that can be treated but never cured, so I'll always be an addict, living out my life in the shadow of relapse, forever in a constant struggle with the temptation to stick a needle in my arm for no more valid a reason than that's what an addict does. When that happens—when I use—I'll ruin everything I earned, built, or acquired in my sobriety. I'll start stealing again, first from my job, which I'll promptly lose, and then from everyone else. No one—friend, family member, or foe—will be able to trust me out of sight. I'll make those who love me cry—again. My mother will cloak herself in denial at first, unwilling to believe that I'm at it yet again. Then she'll lose herself in prayer as reality slaps her in the face—again—and my brothers will recoil with disgust at the sight of me while my sisters shrink with shame at the mention of my name.

Right now I feel pretty good. I make tons of money, much of which I donate to poor. I chair several committees and am very active in community affairs. I have a beautiful wife (we're expecting our thirty-ninth child around Christmastime), and last night I had dinner with President Obama (third time this month) to discuss the concerns of inner city youth.

But it won't last; none of it will last because I'm an addict, see? I've got this incurable disease inside me and sooner or later it will return to the surface to take, ruin, and destroy everything. It will kill everyone close to me and everyone distant from me—and then it will kill me. That's what disease does. That's what makes it disease.

And even if it doesn't come back—even if I never hear from it again, I'll know it's there, that it's in me and will never go away. And just knowing that will rob my mind of peace and deny my spirit rest. The fear of relapse will never diminish or fade. It will forever linger just beyond the surface, mocking my every achievement and overshadowing my every accomplishment. I'll never know that full measure of joy, never realize accomplishment. I'll never realize true and lasting victory.

Because I'm an addict. I'll always be an addict. I'll die an addict.

And keeping it on the "I": I didn't want to be an addict anymore.

CHAPTER EIGHT

When the memory of my last relapse comes to visit me (as it often does) it strikes me almost funny that I hosted a recovery group that discussed social issues and our lack of the skills needed to deal with them soberly. Funny, because it was my own ignorance in two critical areas of social intercourse—relationships and finances—that led to my downfall.

Of course we discussed relationships in the Social Dysfunction and Healing phase. The impact of the men's addiction on the lives of the women they loved was a topic of inexhaustible content. The primary purpose of the phase II group was to explore the ramifications of drug culture in all social arenas, including professional, political, and recreational. Somehow, though, the discussion almost always circled back to the relational, an individual's love life and the harm done to it via his addiction. For the most part I was able to keep the group on course. I have to confess, however, that the subject of love lost or broken by disease fascinated me no end since by that time I had been an addict for what seemed an eternity and couldn't honestly remember when I'd been in a relationship of substance—only one or two of convenience.

The lesson seemed the same with each individual story shared:

keep your sobriety and you'll keep your woman. We arrived at that conclusion without fail. Drug addiction was the source, the very heart of our inability to stay committed and faithful to our significant others. Take away the drugs and you take away the lying, the cheating, the pilfering, the problem.

It seemed almost magical in its simplicity, the inarguable cure to every relational ill from infidelity to abuse. Never mind that it was complete and utter foolishness, that the eradication of drug abuse was just the beginning of the healing process and not the end.

The problem was that our discussions focused so fully on the scourge of addiction in our lives that we never to any significant length talked about life after the scourge was removed. We didn't spend enough time discussing how to behave in a committed relationship, how to be a faithful husband or boyfriend *beyond* not getting high. When I consider these were subjects for which I had no training, no study, and no expertise, I'm forced to admit how sadly unqualified I was to head a recovery group after all.

And so in my own relationship—in my marriage—I was, to put it charitably, not a good husband; to put it more precisely, I was a miserable excuse for a spouse. I think of those first months following my release from Rahway, a clean, sober, cocky model of recovery. I wasn't handsome in the strictest sense of the word, but I looked good, garnering more than my share of attention from the opposite sex. I was smart, funny, charming (even as an addict I'd been smart and funny), and most of all determined to stay drug free.

A major rule for one's successful recovery (and there are many, *all* of which are major) is that one has to be selfish in its pursuit. Essentially that means that nothing is more important than our commitment to sobriety; nothing and no one comes before or matters more than our staying clean and sober. I had preached that one over and over and believed it without question. A life without sobriety is impossible and sobriety is elusive and flighty, requiring undivided attention and undistracted, selfish pursuit.

The thing about selfishness, however, is that it refuses to be restricted to a single area or aspect of one's life. A person who practices selfishness in any part of his life becomes a selfish person, the attribute spilling over into his *entire* life. Selfishness makes us arrogant and inconsiderate and turns us into self-important jackasses without our even realizing it. At many recovery meetings I remember applauding the testimony of many featured speakers who exhibited selfishness as though it were a badge of courage. I remember one such testimony in particular:

"Hi, my name is Carl and I'm an alcoholic. As of last Saturday I've been sober for eight months." *Applause, applause.* "Last Tuesday it all nearly went down the tubes. That's when I received the papers finalizing my divorce. All of a sudden it hit me how much I was gonna miss Judy. Sure it was a bad marriage; all we did was fight about everything under the sun. But we had our good times, too. I mean, underneath all the nagging and complaining she was a good person and I missed her.

"So I'm sitting there looking at those papers and feeling sorry for myself and just like that I start thinking about how good a shot of bourbon would taste." *Commiserate mumbling in the audience.* "Naturally I called my sponsor, but his cell was off—he wasn't answering. So I went over to his house because I really need to talk to this guy before I did something really stupid.

"Anyway, I get to his house and his wife tells me he's working a double shift at his job—that's why he couldn't answer when I called. I guess she could see on my face that I was in a bad way, so she asks if I wanted to talk…"

Carl went on to confess that what started as the sharing of

his loneliness to a sympathetic listener fell into an act of betrayal and adultery between a sponsor's charge and his wife. Larry, the offended sponsor, was arriving home as Carl was leaving. The two spoke briefly, concern and then suspicion registering on Larry's face as Carl grew guilty and evasive and his wife grew scarce. He did not confess to the infidelity but said he could feel his sponsor's glare in the wake of his hasty departure.

"I don't have to tell you that I'm feeling much worse now than when I set out." Carl complains and receives more sympathetic murmuring from his listeners. "Guilty as sin. I mean, by now I didn't just *want* that drink; I *needed* it, know what I mean?" *Moans and groans among the crowd assured Carl we did.* "Next thing you know, I'm at the High Life, this neighborhood bar where I used to hang out." *Emphatic gasps all over.* "I'm just standing there wrestling with myself. I mean, eight months of clean time and I'm ready to just toss it—just like that, you know?"

Carl didn't "toss" his eight months' sobriety. One of the bar patrons, a man to whom Carl apparently owed money, approached Carl to remind him of the outstanding debt. Carl didn't divulge the amount he owed but said the patron—who was a tad inebriated—offered to reduce the total to the price of a couple of drinks. According to Carl, he was looking at this "drunk" who suddenly had come to represent every evil threat imaginable to Carl's sobriety and indeed to his life, and then he was looking at the poor guy on the bar floor where Carl's right hook had deposited him. Then, as is usually the case in taverns, the act of violence became contagious. Someone else hit someone and the place erupted in a melee of flying fists, shouted obscenities, spilled drinks, and breaking furniture.

"Don't know how I got out of there without getting hurt—or drunk." *Chuckles all around.* "But my higher power didn't bring me this far—eight months sober—just to let me blow it all in some dive. I mean, I feel as though he deliberately trashed that place just to keep me from picking up. I still miss that ex of mine, but I can miss her sober just like I can miss her drunk. Anyway, thanks for letting me share, and oh yeah, I'm looking for a new sponsor, if anyone's interested."

A rousing round of applause for Carl, resounding throughout the interior of the VFW banquet hall. Laughter, some cheers and even a few whistles peppered the ovation as we showed our approval for a fellow sufferer who against the odds had managed to maintain his sobriety. In the back of my mind, however, I couldn't help nursing the conviction that our "hero" Carl should have taken the drink. An innocent sponsor's marriage, an innocent drunk's jaw along with a bar full of other innocent drunks plus furnishings would have been better off if he'd simply taken the drink. That he could look upon the chaos and insanity he'd caused as a personal victory while at the same time crediting it all to divine intervention was an offensive shock to my conscience and a crime against all that was right and reasonable.

He should have taken the drink.

But of course I didn't say it. In truth, I didn't even think it. Carl had managed to not drink and to him and to me and to everyone else in recovery that was all there was.

And with that attitude—with that mind-set—I married Debra. I didn't know how to reconcile the selfish pursuit of recovery with the pursuit of a successful marriage. We didn't cover that in Social Dysfunction and Healing.

It wasn't that I didn't love Debra; I did, inasmuch as someone in the selfish pursuit of recovery is able to love anyone. It was my first marriage. I was forty-five at the time, so of course I didn't want it to fail. Debra was a sweet and stunningly attractive woman, just under a month my senior. The first time we got together she actually asked me out. We went to Red Lobster and ate steak and shrimp while I regaled her of tales from my past, leaving little out without shame or regret. I was to all appearances proud to be an ex-con in recovery.

Unfortunately my "recovery before all else" attitude that made me appear strong and determined as a bachelor was not as attractive an attribute in me as a married man. It wasn't that I was thoughtless or unfaithful. I treated Debra well, never spoke unkindly to her or even entertained the notion of infidelity—at least not at length. I also got along well with her sons, Mark and Dale. I added to the house finances and refurnished the house with the employee discount I received at my job.

I thought I was being a good husband, but I was only going through the motions, playing at marriage. Debra was not the priority in my life that she wanted to be and should have been. What I didn't know at the time was that I was following an expected program of recovery: finding work, paying my taxes, going to meetings, and getting married—all the things that mark a complete and successful life of sobriety, all the things normal people do. Neither Debra nor I knew that she was only part of my recovery process: a component of my sobriety and not a component of me. If I loved her, it was a sorry imitation of love—an impotent and fruitless leftover of selfishness.

And then there was the matter of money. Another of the social skills we failed to adequately explore in our prized prison recovery classes was the skill for handling one's personal finances. When I went away in 1985, only the affluent possessed credit cards, or so it seemed to me. When I was paroled in '97, everyone seemed to have them. Within a couple of months of my release—when I started working, thus sending my social security number circulating through the monetary system—I received at least one credit card application every week. The loan companies were hot to have my signature on their bottom lines and my neck in their nooses. They were even sending me checks made out in my name, ready to cash and spend. For a while I was a good steward, making above-minimum payments on or ahead of time and earning increased credit limits. Unfortunately a single man's spending discipline doesn't carry over into marriage any more successfully than his attitude for recovery does, and almost before I realized it, I—we—were in deep trouble with the finance companies. This caused a great deal of friction between Debra and me. We quarreled over the bills incessantly. At one point I even took a second job at a supermarket in Hamilton Township, but it seemed the harder I worked, the deeper in debt we sank until at the suggestion of my employer at the furniture company, I filed for bankruptcy. Debra found this a degrading and humiliating failure, which I just didn't understand. I saw it as a way out from under the ever-increasing weight of debt. But Debra continued to display such a deep and abiding shame for Chapter 7 bankruptcy that I began to think that there must have been an insurmountable stigma attached to the economic remedy that I couldn't perceive, that we had had been marked with a scarlet letter to make socioeconomic pariahs of us. An oppressive pall fell over me as I considered this. I brooded, grew depressed …

And took the first drink of my last relapse.

CHAPTER NINE

Relapse is a more complicated and involved process than many know, usually occurring in steps rather than as a single and sudden sobriety-ending act. In the meetings we discuss "relapse behavior," our wrong responses to life issues that inevitably lead us back to substance abuse. Conventional wisdom holds that an addict's emotional development ceases at the age at which he became a substance abuser; the younger he is at the beginning of his addiction, the more immature he remains throughout.

While the mature adult is aware of the transient nature of the more uncomfortable or "negative" emotions like rejection or fear, the addict is not content to wait them out. It's either drown them or drown *in* them. Although his relapse isn't considered official until he drinks, pops, smokes, snorts, or injects, he has effectively relapsed when he allows life issues to loom larger and darker in his mind than he believes he has the ability to surmount.

Because I was a cocaine addict, my relapse was further complicated by the fact that it came in a bottle rather than a bag. There is often a strange dichotomy between alcoholics and narcotics abusers; neither accepts the other's condition as a legitimate addiction, therefore neither accepts the other as legimately ill.

When addicts call alcoholics "drunks," the term is more often a reference to social lowliness than infirmity, and for the most part, alcoholics see drug addicts as thugs and criminals. The twelve principles of Narcotics Anonymous declare alcohol is a drug, and alcoholics generally agree. But the separation remains, despite their acceptance of each other's company in combined recovery meetings.

I attended both AA and NA meetings. While my addiction was pretty much exclusively to cocaine, I was as incapable of taking a drink as any alcoholic. I said as much at the AA meetings when I was asked to share. For me, alcohol is a gateway drug. During the thirty years of my addiction, I'd had many "clean seasons," short-lived periods of recovery. Each and every time I relapsed began with a drink and ended just weeks, or more often just days, later with me sitting in some shooting gallery with a needle in my arm. I could always find a legitimate reason for that first one: "Just a cold beer to beat the heat" or "I had a tough day at work. I deserve just one to unwind." It was a crock, of course. I don't know who it was that insisted you can lie to others but you can't lie to yourself, but I'd bet the farm he was no addict—then again, maybe he was, lying to himself even then. With heartfelt statements like "I can quit any time I want" and "So help me, if I get out of this one, I'll never use again" echoing eternally in my history, I can attest to the truth of self-delusion.

When I took that drink during my troubles with Debra, however, it was different. The lies I told myself were the same as always: "under pressure," "help me relax," yadda, yadda. But this time they didn't provide me with the comfort I needed to dwell in this failure. Still, comfortable or not, I didn't worry about things like the unforgivable disgrace of bankruptcy when I had a few drinks in me, so ...

I don't recall actually quitting the job in Hamilton. Like my post with New Directions years before, I simply stopped going. Soon after and for the first time in the four years since I was hired at the furniture company, I began to arrive at work late and perform in mediocre fashion. The first time my supervisor confronted me about this he expressed genuine concern, asking if I were all right, if I were having problems at home, if I needed time off or other assistance. The next meeting—this time with the manager—was conducted more in the way of my being given an ultimatum: shape up or ship out. At both meetings I assured my superiors that I was and would be all right. At both meetings I was just a little intoxicated and was pretty sure they knew.

I was already shooting cocaine again when they caught me stealing at the job. I don't know exactly when it happened. As I said, relapse is a complicated matter. I had grown tired of booze, weary of the stumbling, dreary inebriation it inflicted. Alcohol didn't have that jet-pack, escape-velocity high cocaine provided, didn't make your heart pound and your blood race. Coke made you bright-eyed, bushy-tailed, alert. Coke made you *fly*.

They caught me red-handed, in the act, loading company property into my car. I wouldn't confess to the attempted theft, instead offering some broken, rambling explanation for the guilty spectacle before them. In addition to the increased cardiac activity and wings, coke also makes you stupid to the point of complete incoherence. Then they made me the proverbial offer I couldn't refuse: leave the premises immediately on my own or in police custody.

Well, I wasn't *that* stupid.

I was unemployed about four months when Debra put me out. In all honesty I never really felt a true sense of ownership or belonging at her house; it had been a home made by Debra and her first husband. Despite my material contributions there, it never felt like my own. While I was sober and involved in my selfish pursuit of recovery, I'd been able to ignore the sense that I was not in charge there, that in many ways I was an outsider. Now that I was not contributing financially, though, my status came up to slap my face fiercely and repeatedly.

And poor Debra. She hadn't bargained for this. When she married me, I was clean and sober, gainfully employed—a "catch." Now I was collecting unemployment while I "looked" for another job and using almost daily. Cocaine is an expensive indulgence. My income had been reduced to bimonthly payments of $700 and I was "banging" no less than $100 a day in powder. The math didn't work for Debra, especially when money earmarked for paying bills or stashed around the house for emergencies began to disappear. At the beginning of our relationship, I had, from the secure loft of my sobriety, told Debra countless horror stories about my life as an outlaw, regaled her with tales of my underground exploits with a casual, almost detached regard for the man I had been. Now all those stories came slamming back to her as a grim portent of the hell that was about to break loose in her life—and in her house.

And she was having none of it. I remember the argument we had when she told me she wanted me out. Her sons, thankfully, kept a watchful distance, saying nothing but maintaining a conspicuous presence for their mother's protection. I know they liked me for the person I was when they met me. Only now as I write this does it strike me how difficult it must have been for them.

Debra was never one to hide her feelings of anger or disappointment, nor was she quick to pardon those responsible for those feelings (especially husbands). She had on occasion opened up to me about the transgressions of the first man she married. Now I had become as he: inadequate, insufficient, a loser. Though those were not her words, it was nonetheless her sentiment. She had a way of speaking to me, a way of looking at me that let me know that I had descended to a level somewhere just beneath her contempt and just above her loathing. I'd first heard that tone and saw that look the day I brought up the subject of bankruptcy. Naturally seeing it again now made me defensive and angry. I started to crow about all I'd done for her, the money I'd spent to replace the worn and shabby furniture in her house, the overall quality of life there that I had served to improve despite my financial troubles. For a while we faced off on the front porch, each claiming sole responsibility for any good that went into or came out of our association. The confrontation never came anywhere close to violence. Nevertheless someone summoned the police, who of course told me that I had to leave. It was, after all, Debra's house.

A number of neighbors were on hand to witness my eviction and with that ignominious send-off, I walked away from my marriage and made my way back to the streets of Trenton. As I hurry through this portion of my story, I see that I failed to mention that just before things started to get bad with my credit, I had leased a new car—my first new car ever—and had it repossessed (another personal economic upheaval Debra was not at all pleased with) just a few months later.

I should also mention that I made an attempt to get clean and save my marriage by enrolling in a rehab in South Philadelphia. I got high there every day and when they kicked me out, the program director offered me a job selling crack for him on the street. As I was unfamiliar with the City of Brotherly Love and more than a little apprehensive hustling in an area where I'd likely be deemed an intruder, I declined. That was the summer of 2001.

Two months later the World Trade Center was devastated by terrorists.

I guess it was a good year for devastation.

CHAPTER TEN

Many years ago my youngest sister, Stephanie, made the most disturbing prophesy regarding me. She told me that God had His Hand on my life, that He would call me to His service and that I would serve him mightily. Those, as I recall, are almost her exact words.

It disturbed me because I didn't know what to make of it. I wasn't a stranger to the church, nor was I its closest acquaintance. I didn't care about church one way or the other. Attending as a boy was law in my mother's house, but as I said, when I got old enough to stop going, I stopped going. I returned after getting out of prison only because, like marrying Debra, it was part of my recovery process. It wouldn't be fair to say I didn't enjoy it more than I did as a boy. As a sober and mature adult, I liked church well enough. I even had fun as a member of the pastor's outreach ministry and singing in the men's choir. Again, though, I was only going through the motions, doing what was expected of me and making no personal or spiritual investment as I went.

Steph—as I suppose is the case with the youngest sisters of the oldest brothers—had a way of getting inside me. Things she'd say to or about me affected me more deeply and remained with me far longer than things said by any of my other siblings. It wasn't that she was wiser or more insightful than the others, but she was the youngest of the sisters, her eyes a little starrier, her regard for me a tad more worshipful. If there was anything about me worthy of admiration, Steph was the one to find it. I lent no true value to her "prophesy" about me serving God and I didn't know it at the time, but that baby sister of mine had—perhaps merely by virtue of speaking it—planted something inside me. When I think of it now I can almost believe it was Steph who had on some hidden level of my awareness at least partially revealed the gods of addiction to me.

And for having shared that, I'm ready to talk about them now, before I go into the final desperate years of my life as a drug addict, before reliving the betrayals and revealing my crimes, before describing for you the squalid conditions in which I resided and the toll it took on my health. I'm ready to talk about them.

I know now that they were with me—in me—for a long time. How long I'm not certain, but I'm ready to believe now that as I moved away from the church—as I moved away from God—they moved in, creating disorder and dysfunction.

And *addiction*? I once thought so. When I came to accept the reality of their existence and presence inside me, I believed they were responsible, that they'd made me an addict. I know now that they never possessed the power to do that, that drug abuse was a choice I had to make freely so that they would be increased and strengthened, able to gain the subtle influence over my life that *was* their power.

They were demons, evil spirits, devils. They dwelled deep inside me, occupying that dark empty place in me that should not have been dark and empty. Manipulating my emotions, perverting my perceptions, infusing my motives with selfishness.

And my addiction?

My addiction was the banquet table at which these usurpers of my life feasted, nourishing and strengthening themselves on a fare of my relationships, my self-respect, the trust and good will of all who cared for me, and eleven years of my freedom.

My addiction was the altar of worship upon which I sacrificed my marriage, my employment, my health, my peace, and my joy, a burning pyre on which I presented my hopes, my dreams, and my future, elevating the dark ones dwelling inside me from mere demons to gods.

But I was not supposed to know they were there, that they existed. Their greatest strength was in their undetected presence, their anonymity. Hidden, they could promote the destructive fire of my addiction as sickness while reaping my floundering soul as tribute, but when Stephanie shared with me her "vision" of me serving God, I believe her words had the effect of a light whisper of a breeze moving a veil ever so slightly, briefly exposing what it concealed. Just a glimpse—not enough to identify them or even guess what they were. Just enough to know they were there. With me. In me. But it wasn't enough to stop me. My dark odyssey into the world of the addicted and the damned happened nonetheless. Still, in the midst of it all, in the worst of it all, at the bottom of it all—in my heart I knew. I just knew.

It wasn't sickness. It wasn't disease.

It was *them*.

It was the gods. And they didn't speak to me, didn't encourage me in my self-destruction. They preferred to simply watch, undetected and inconspicuous. It didn't serve them to be known. But they couldn't help reacting with subtle, shielded smiles to my suffering, and I was aware of their malicious glee. I never heard or saw or even sense their evil enjoyment. *I just knew.*

And so I could never reconcile myself with the idea of my

addiction as some incurable malady. I had learned and taught it, argued and defended it; maybe on some level I even believed it. But I couldn't make peace with it, because I always knew about *them*. However peripherally, *I always knew.*

In these, the better days of my life, I think of my baby sister and her heartfelt belief that I would become a servant of God. Then I think of the broken path upon which I tread almost immediately after, and I wonder if that were God's plan for me all along or if perhaps he was obliged to alter His design on my life to accommodate the wrong choices I made. Did I choose the longest, most twisted road I could find only to arrive at exactly where He always wanted me?

But in the fall of 2001, as I wandered, a homeless cokehead out to score by whatever means I could, those questions were years away, much further down that long twisted road I had chosen. Long before such life-altering ruminations would occur to me I would encounter heartache, fear, violence, loneliness, near-crippling infirmity, and near-death, lying immobile and helpless in a filthy basement, my life draining out of me from an accidental overdose ... with the gods of addiction mocking me all the way.

CHAPTER ELEVEN

Hello, my name is Mitch and I'm an addict.

That is to say, I've faced the truth about my addiction. Walking the streets without place or prospects has a way of forcing reality upon you, making you see the world as it truly is and yourself for what you truly are.

Oh, I can go into rehab—again. I can get clean and sober for months and even years at a time, attend meetings, counsel individuals or even groups in recovery. When all is said and done, however, I'm an addict. It always comes back to that—it always comes *down* to that.

Actually, it's really liberating, confessing this dismal truth. It takes away the denial, the self-delusion. It makes you honest, believe it or not, because it gives you a guilt-free hand to move as the addiction demands, to do what you have to. It even takes some of the shame out of the many other truths you come to learn about yourself.

Like being a thief. All addicts are thieves, committed to keeping the addiction alive at someone else's expense. I'd lost my taste for armed robbery, though: too repercussive. Still, the finances must be acquired and I've neither the temperament nor the constitution to hold down a job...

(*my feet hurt*)

...so I occupy myself with petty crime. I've tried the various street hustles but lacked the patience or the aptitude required for any appreciable measure of success. As I said earlier, cocaine is like rocket fuel; it makes you run (*although I've been running considerably less in months past—my feet hurt*), so I visit the stores—supermarkets, pharmacies, and the like—resorting to the means for generating revenue with which I'm most comfortable. I get in and get out. Everything from electronics to tools to cosmetics to over-the-counter drugs are concealed under my clothing, items I can peddle to the patrons at local bars and even to other stores. It's a slow hustle at a quick pace and with the briefest of profit margins, so in order to support an addiction as demanding as mine, I'm at it all day long all over town.

I'm an addict. My appearance is pathetic. I was a lean, well-defined, and well-groomed figure of a man when I was released from Rahway almost six years ago. Today I'm almost skeletal to behold. I had to punch another hole in my belt to keep my trousers from falling down. My cheeks are sunken, my smile dull (recently I lost a tooth biting into a peach), my eyes wide, and my gaze darting. My personal hygiene is just shy of nonexistent; sometimes I offend myself.

(*and my feet really hurt*)

I live in a boardinghouse with other addicts (drug den, crack house, shooting gallery—pick a name) on the West Side. Presently I'm still collecting unemployment, but that's soon to expire and unless I can work out something with Marty Redman, my heroin-addicted landlord, my residency there will expire as well. But that's not a "now" worry. Addicts care only about right now, and right now I'm covered.

I don't see my family much these days. I miss them, especially Mom. I go to visit on occasion—when I can use a decent meal or have gone longer without showering and changing than even I can stand. I put up with Mom's pleas that I seek help yet again to get clean, but it's becoming increasingly clear to her that I'm not interested. I just don't see the point. As I said at the start of this chapter, I've come to terms with the fact that I'm an addict.

Sometimes when I go to the house, my sister Brenda is there. A recovering addict herself with better than a dozen years clean, Brenda reads me the riot act about bringing my miserable self to Mom's. She really lets me have it, a relentless assault of insults and maledictions. She even castigates Mom for enabling me, complaining that as long as she lets me in the house—as long as she continues to be my "safety net"—I'll never even consider getting clean. Brenda is a tough one to ignore; she knows which buttons to push and has no compunctions about pushing them. Having Mom's hurt-filled eyes on me is hard enough without having to hear from Brenda what a low-life I am. But again, it's just one of those truths one comes to accept with that one major truth: I'm an addict. It's the way of my life to get rebuked, rebuffed, maligned, disowned, and shunned, exploited and abused, looked over and overlooked, beaten, jailed, discarded, and forgotten.

And to get sick. Plantar warts and calluses dig their homes into the balls and soles of my feet so I can't run anymore—can barely walk, taking hours to cover distances I used to clear in minutes, seconds. Searing, unbearable pain results with every step. The cocaine does nothing to blunt the acute agony—still it remains my number-one priority. I lumber, amble, inch my way along to my next score, anticipating the moment when I can take my full weight off my hurting, howling dogs long enough to have a pointless and unsatisfying affair with a coke-filled hypo—assuming my local dealer doesn't sell me baking soda or something far worse. That's another ugly truth about being an addict. We get cheated. We get played.

And we stop. Not using—living. Addicts don't die. We just stop.

CHAPTER TWELVE

Cocaine makes you want to run. But I can't run anymore. So I sat in exam room number four in my backless gown, waiting for the doctor to arrive, give my hurting feet the once-over, recommend I make an appointment with a podiatrist, and send me on my way. He won't offer me anything for the pain, though, not so much as an aspirin. When it comes to giving medication to junkies, I guess the word in New Jersey is "don't."

I wasn't here for meds anyway. I came because it was late December, bitter cold outside, and the pain in my feet had become so excruciating, I wrestled with a perverse impulse to hack them off at the ankles and hobble along on the stumps. Walking—if that's what you choose to call my agonized shuffle—actually brought tears to my eyes. A month or so before, I'd been able to exact minor relief from the pain by taking a razor to the circles of hardened skin on the soles of my feet and shaving them off. That didn't work anymore and they hurt all the time, even when I was lying down and my weight wasn't pressing down on them.

The examination room was cold, but I was in no hurry to leave. I sat quietly, tempted to lie prone on the sterile sheet of paper covering the vinyl surface of the exam table and close my eyes.

More than anything I wanted to sleep. As uncomfortable as I felt, I could just lie down right there and sleep.

That's what I really wanted: a night's sleep in a nice clean hospital. I knew I wouldn't get that here, though. A couple of weeks before I'd tried at a different hospital. All I got was the exam, the recommendation, and the boot. The doctor had even paraded a group of med students by my bed, describing the condition of my feet to them in medical jargon. I felt humiliated, like a specimen.

My unemployment had expired last month. I told Redman when I made my last rent payment that my income stream had dried up. He was pretty decent about it at the time. He actually said I could drop a ten on him every couple of days and go on living in the basement.

Bear in mind, I'm not talking about a basement apartment— just the basement. You should know also that it's where I'd been living all the time, ever since being ousted from my marital bed in Levittown. So what Red was offering was for my living situation in his building to remain as it had always been at a reduced rate. That may not sound like much, but I was never one for living on the street, especially in the winter. At $150 a month, Red's basement was the best offer in town. I'd found a perfectly good mattress and box spring someone had put out for trash pick-up, brought it back, and set it up on a frame of cinder blocks. Quite a comedown from the furniture company, but that's the way it is in the life of a junkie.

Anyway, Red's boardinghouse was across town from where I was at the moment—which was roughly equivalent to saying it was at the summit of Mount Everest, given the condition of my feet tonight. I'd been out hustling all evening, ostensibly to drop a ten on Red. It had been a couple of weeks since our new rental arrangement went into effect, and I knew he'd be at the door with his hand out when I came in. I was able to come up with the money a few hours earlier but had used it to score. Junkies are not noted for their discipline. If financial obligations aren't met before opportunities arise, it's likely they won't be met at all.

Sometime around midnight it had started to rain. I could feel my sneakers shrinking on my hurting feet. Hustling had been enough of an ordeal when they were dry. I knew that I'd never make it to the West Side tonight, so I ambled over to the emergency room at Helene Fuld Medical Center. The nurse at registration didn't exhibit a great deal of sympathy for my condition and resisted accepting me as an emergency case; she relented, however, and took my information when I insisted I couldn't walk. Maybe, since it seemed a slow night for ER activity, she thought it would be as easy to let the doctor toss me. In any case, I didn't expect much. I had no money and no insurance; my ailment called for a specialist who undoubtedly was not available, and let's not forget I'm a junkie, at the very bottom of the food chain.

It seemed I'd been in that room a long time. I was growing wearier, sleepier by the minute. It struck me that this was not how emergency rooms work, then I reminded myself that I was not an emergency case. I was about to give in to my earlier impulse to lie down on that cold, uncomfortable table in that cold, uncomfortable room in my backless, tail-exposed gown and drift away in uncomfortable slumber, when I spotted him in the doorway.

He was not a doctor unless hospital dress code had undergone a drastic change. His attire was black save for that slot of white, his cleric's collar. A gold-tone badge hung on a chain around his neck. I didn't like the badge. A wide smile and bright brown eyes illuminated a face the color of night. I didn't like the smile either.

"My brother, our Lord and Savior, Jesus Christ has sent me to bring you glad tidings of hope and joy," he announced cheerily and I thought, *You gotta be kidding. Nobody talks like that.*

"The doctor ain't here," I mumbled stupidly. It was all I could think to say.

"Oh, my brother, but the doctor is here." The insufferably cheerful intruder corrected me. "He's here and He's now. He's ready and able to remove all illness, affliction, and infirmity. He knows the desires of your heart, my brother. He knows your needs and he's ready to supply every one.

"I've come to tell you that our Lord Jesus loves you and can make you whole again. He can bring you peace and fulfillment like no drug ever could. He can bring you up from the ground, chase away the demons and restore you to fullness."

I felt a surge of anger at his words. What does he know about me and drugs—not that one look at me wouldn't tell the tale, but what does he know? And what was that about bringing me up from the ground? Was that some reference to me living in a basement? And all that talk about wholeness and fulfillment and ... and ... *demons*

Then the anger was gone as quickly as it had come, a startling sense of apprehension taking its place. I felt exposed, more exposed than even the flimsy cotton gown I wore permitted. I drew my ashen, knobby knees together, forgetting for the moment my hurting feet.

"Mister—"

"Chaplain." The smiling man again corrected me, stepping further into the exam room and extending his hand in greeting. "Chaplain Tommy Young."

He must have been at least six feet six. The tiny examination room shrank all the more for his entrance. I shook his big hand, distracted by his smile and a feeling of something else that seemed to enter the room with him: a feeling of well-being, a sense of peace.

I knew about chaplains. Years ago, long before I went to Rahway,

I went to the hospital—this hospital, as a matter of fact—after taking a beating from some guys I'd cheated out of three hundred dollars in buy money. They tore into me, trounced me soundly enough to collapse a lung, though I didn't know the extent of my injuries at the time. I knew only that I had to sleep sitting up because I could barely breathe when I lay down. After two days of watching me this way, Mom said simply that if I didn't go to the hospital I'd likely die before another sunrise.

They admitted me with a collapsed lung and pneumonia. That was when I saw a chaplain for the first time. They visit patients' rooms, handing out religious tracts, offering gospel-based encouragement and prayer. I think they are required to record so many such visits to submit to their supervisors so that they can keep their license or badges or whatever. It seemed strange that a chaplain wound be down here in admissions, however—especially since it was unlikely that I would be admitted.

"Chaplain, I..." I started to introduce myself and stopped short, unsure if it made sense to continue. I felt like nobody before this big, smiling chaplain. I didn't have a title. A hundred labels, but no title.

During that year after I admitted to myself that I was a junkie (you'll note I use the term "junkie" now rather than "addict," as the latter is more clinical, denoting hope for recovery), I'd more or less gotten used to the truth that I was a nobody, a loser. Now in the presence of this big dude I felt all the more a nobody, more the loser. I can't explain it even looking back, but I felt even more naked and guilty than I was, my hospital gown as small and inappropriate as a fig leaf.

I don't know if this big guy, this Chaplain Tommy Young could pick up on my discomfiture. It certainly seemed he could. He put his left hand on my shoulder even as his right hand held mine. I looked up at my giant of a visitor. His smile had softened and he seemed all the more imposing for it. At the same time there was something disarming, even soothing about Chaplain Tommy.

"'For I know the thoughts that I think toward you,' says the LORD, 'thoughts of peace and not of evil, to give you a future and a hope.'"

The big man released my hand and stood back, allowing his words to settle over me. "Jeremiah 29:11," he said, and smile grew huge again. "God has sent me to tell you to be of good courage. He has His Hand on your life and a design for your future. He wants you to know he calls you to His service."

My belly flipped in violent response to the big man's words. My mind raced back through the years to Stephanie's similar "prophesy." I didn't get it then and it made less sense to me now. Did I look like someone fit to serve God? Was there something about me that conveyed a quality I didn't know I possessed?

I'm a burned-out junkie with rotting feet. What kind of service could I give? I can barely walk.

'Thoughts for a future and a hope'? *What* future? What *hope*?

My eyelids drooped with weariness. I felt tired—tired and ashamed. I lowered my head and closed my eyes, willing away the fatigue. A dull throbbing began at my temples and then ceased. I drew a breath and opened my eyes.

Chaplain Tommy was gone. I didn't hear or feel him leave; he didn't utter a word of good-bye.

The room had seemed warmer for his intrusion. With his departure, the sterile coldness slowly returned. I shivered, my hands clenching in reaction to the declining temperature and heard the crumple of paper in my grasp. I stared, dazed and wondering at the religious tract Chaplain Tommy evidently had placed in my hand before making his sudden and silent exit.

My belly began to tremble again, as though something in there did not want me to read the pamphlet. Without my dollar-store reading glasses, I had to hold the tract almost at arm's length to make out the small bold print of the title:

The Healing of a Demon-Possessed Man

Then I had to squint to read the smaller print of the text:

> Mark 5:1. So they arrived at the other side of the lake, in the region of the Gerasenes. 2 When Jesus climbed out of the boat, a man possessed by an evil spirit came out from a cemetery to meet him. 3 This man lived among the burial caves and could no longer be restrained, even with a chain. 4 Whenever he was put into the chains and shackles—as he often was—he snapped the chains on his wrists and smashed the shackles. No one was strong enough to subdue him. 5 Day and night he wandered among the burial caves and in the hills, howling and cutting himself with sharp stones...

I stopped, my mind stumbling over the meaning of what I was reading.

This story...this story of a man, a...*(possessed)*...crazy man living in a cemetery, screaming and hurting himself, doing insane, destructive things to himself because he...*(had a demon inside him)*...was sick...crazy and sick.

It hurt my head to read this way—without my cheap glasses. I didn't like what I was reading, either, didn't like the way it made me feel. I crumpled the tract in my fist, thinking to toss it at the stainless steel wastebasket by the door. I raised my hand, measuring the throw ...

Inexplicably I brought the tract down, resting it on my bare thigh. Using the heel of my hand like an iron, I made a fair attempt at smoothing out some of the wrinkles I'd crushed into the paper. I don't know why. I had no intention of reading any more. I didn't like the story, the feelings it stirred, the way the words kept repeating in my head. I didn't like Chaplain Tommy for giving it to me. He shouldn't have been there anyway, bothering the patients while they're waiting to see the doctor.

"Hi, I'm Doctor Patel. You say you're having pain in your feet?"

For the second time in just minutes someone was able to enter that tiny examination room through a door almost within my reach without my noticing. I looked up from the tract I was nursing to the small, dark-hued, white-coated man speaking more to the report in his hand than to me.

"Yeah, Doctor," I answered wearily.

To my surprise, the young Indian intern treated my feet, shaving off the callused flesh and slathering on a soothing balm.

Even more surprising: they let me stay the rest of the night. The doctor ordered I be allowed to remain off my feet until the medication had had time to work. I slept in a clean bed for four hours, ate the breakfast they brought to me, and then left. If the strangeness of the night before came back to me—the complete departure from hospital protocol from admission to release—it all got lost as I made my way back to my West Side digs. Best of all, my feet were feeling pretty good, the best they'd felt in a while.

Later that evening as I was making my rounds, a souped-up Dodge Ram pulled over to the curb near me. The driver, a young man with frizzy blond hair introduced himself to me as Roger, asking if I knew where he could find a few grams of coke. He promised, of course, to take care of me if I set up the buy.

Needless to say, my little basement spot was a hot bed of activity that night. Dealers came, made their sales and went, leaving Roger and me plus a hanger-on or two to abuse cocaine until I thought I'd go into cardiac hyperdrive. I don't know how much my best friend for the evening started out with—quite a lot, to say the least—but he was running on empty by morning.

Sometime during the night, Red came down. Roger gave him forty dollars (my rent for the next week or so). He stayed awhile to indulge with us, as did a few others who lived in the building. From time to time, a female hustler or two would come down to make offers that didn't interest us in the least. Forget what you may have heard about cocaine's effect on the libido. I mean, it may be true when it's used in minor, recreational doses, but for hardcore abusers, the result is quite the opposite; sexual desire is just this side of nonexistent. Even so, however, Roger would provide our would-be concubines with a crumb or two in the interest of sustaining the party atmosphere of the house. Of course during all the spending, I would skim and pocket a ten or a twenty from nearly every transaction Roger made. It was Friday night and I was a hero, the man of the hour.

When Roger left at about ten the next morning (he swore we'd do it again that night and I pretended to believe him), I was glad to see him go. I had almost two hundred dollars of his money stashed away; my night was set. Red was off my back for the rent at least for a little while, and my feet felt fine. The events of Thursday night—Chaplain Tommy's "message from God" and his unsettling pamphlet—were forgotten.

I lay back on the perfectly good mattress I'd found and closed my eyes, contented. If *they* were laughing at me now, I was laughing along with them.

I could run again.

CHAPTER THIRTEEN

The first one in the house to die—to *stop*—was Victor.

You could say that Victor and I were friends. It was a relationship grounded in addiction, mutual desperation, and street-law survival, but in our world you learned to take people as they came; you had little right to expect more.

So, yes, Victor and I shared a friendship—superficial and shaky as it was.

I first met Victor one night shortly after I moved into the Passaic Street boardinghouse. I was returning home from "work," a part-time lifting-and-moving gig I found at a second-hand store roughly two miles up the road. I'd actually gone there to sell a computer I'd scavenged in front of an office building (evidently the management there had upgraded). The store manager didn't want it, however, said it was too old. I guess he saw my disappointment and annoyance for having lugged a CPU hard drive, monitor, keyboard, speakers, and attachments all that way, and he asked if I wanted a job. No doubt he could also see that I was a junkie, someone to be exploited for pocket change and hired me under the table, paying me at the end of the day pretty much whatever he felt like paying. There were two other "employees" like me—junkies performing hard, dirty labor for whatever wages the boss deemed appropriate. He rarely gave us more than $50 a day.

Bear in mind I was collecting unemployment at the time. The $700 checks I received every two weeks made for a nice day of eating, drinking, drugging, and other forms of debauchery plus the rent. By the morning of the next day I was almost always broke with two weeks to go before my next "nice day."

Victor was sitting on the porch of the once-handsome brownstone with two of the building's other residents, Vonnette and Leon. Vonnette had about as loud and profane a mouth as one would expect of the crackhead she was. Leon, her dope-fiend paramour, loved her nevertheless (again you have to consider the world and its inhabitants when considering concepts like love and friendship).

The two were together all the time—you almost never saw one without the other—and when they were together they were arguing, him complaining about her nagging and infidelity, and her disparaging his carnal prowess. Tonight's conversational knock-down-drag-out was no exception. At first glance I assumed Victor—sitting quietly on the steps—was enjoying the nasty exchange between our feuding neighbors, but then I saw he was actually grimacing in response to some inner discomfort he apparently was experiencing.

I made my way up onto the porch, giving Victor a cursory nod as I passed. In my arms I carried the six-pack of beer I would imbibe as I prepared my "main course," the gram of coke in my pocket for injection. Fortunately I didn't have to agonize over having to spend any of my hard-earned money on food; Curt, the boss at my "job," had sprung for lunch for his off-the-books crew. Considering what he was saving in labor costs, it was the least he could do.

Victor and I locked gazes as I walked by—actually his eyes went first to the bag in my arms then to my face. I don't think there was anything in my expression that invited Victor to join me, but he did anyway, rising to enter the house behind me. A few minutes later we were sitting together in the kitchen getting acquainted over two of my beers.

It's unfortunate—sad how little we get to know each other in that life. Most of our "friendships" are built on a mutual addiction to the same drug of choice: heroin addicts associate with other heroin addicts, likewise crackheads with crackheads and so on. Victor was a heroin addict who somewhere along the way had contracted hepatitis C (I don't remember how I learned that; I'm fairly certain he didn't tell me). He was a light-skinned brother with black curly hair and dark eyes. It wasn't hard to imagine women found Victor attractive in his early, innocent years. But those years were long lost. Now his skin was sallow, his frame emaciated by opiate abuse and the disease that was disintegrating his liver by the moment. He had less than a half-dozen teeth remaining, and his hands, after serving for years as injection sites, were swollen and spotted.

I liked Victor. When I offered him a beer that first night, he took it with gushing gratitude, as though I was the most generous human being he ever met. In that house I probably was, although I made no offer nor harbored any intention of sharing the gram in my pocket.

Mostly I guess Victor was lonely. So was I. I thought about Debra and her sons a lot. My mother and my siblings and their kids were constantly on my mind. I also thought about the friends I made at Wayne Avenue Baptist Church, especially the brothers in the male chorus. I enjoyed singing with them (I don't mind telling you I carry a tune fairly well).

Sometimes I can barely stand myself when those memories come back to me, memories of how I let everyone down. That's the number-one reason junkies don't delve deeply into one another's past. No one wants to talk about the things that make them feel guilty, things that make them wish they could just stop living.

Victor and I started to hang out together. During the day we'd hit the streets, hustling, drinking, "visiting" the stores. Victor wasn't much for shoplifting, but he had my back—more or less—as lookout and it was good to have him along for the ride. We didn't spend a great deal of time together. A heroin addict, Victor was naturally drawn to his own kind but was always on hand when my unemployment checks came. Believe it or not, I didn't mind. It was good to have his company, however ulterior his motive. As I said, I liked Victor.

We had our first and only fight on the last night of Victor's life. It was my fault. We'd been hanging out a little over a year. My unemployment had stopped coming by then, and it had been a while since I'd made a decent score. On that night Victor had helped me sell a cordless telephone I'd boosted. But the profit was smaller than I'd hoped and rather than share it with Victor, I spent it all on myself.

It started as a shouting match in my basement spot. Victor was really upset. I wasn't worried; I was sure I could take him if it came to that. But I grew increasingly annoyed at his threats. As far as I was concerned, he should have had no problem allowing me this one selfish indulgence after all I'd shared with him. I told him as much; he just looked at me as if I was crazy. This made me even angrier and I told him to get out. Cursing, Victor left and I thought no more of it.

I don't know how long it was before he returned. Time holds little significance for junkies; there's only now. We while away the hours in back lots, abandoned buildings, and alleys. Years may pass without our having left the same six-block radius. Time races away from us while we remain suspended and—believe it or not, *preserved* in our addiction. I know that sounds insane, but it's true.

Yes, addiction wears you out, dries you up, and breaks you down. Addiction mutates you, makes you nocturnal and ugly, eventually kills you. In the meantime, however, addiction holds you, sort of salt-cures you in your rotting ugliness. Addiction will make a thirty-year-old look fifty and insanely, keep him looking that way for fifty years. As I said, for a junkie there is only now.

I glanced up to the sound of descending footfalls on the basement stairs. I saw the metal pole (at least eight feet long, the thin, insulated type through which electrical wires are strung) in Victor's hands before his face appeared. I got quickly to my feet, alarm bells going off in my head.

"I want my money, Mitch." He was enraged. Obviously he'd gone off to talk himself into this move. It wouldn't have surprised me to learn that one or two others in the house were on hand to bolster his courage.

The verbal exchange was brief and pointless: him demanding money I didn't have and would not have surrendered if I did and me ordering him out of my place. Then the inevitable escalation: I was careful to time his swing, jumping back just as he brought the pole around. It missed me but nearly demolished the 32-inch television set someone discarded that proved to be in perfect working condition. The end of the pole clipped the set low, knocking off two of the knobs, one of them the channel changer. Infuriated, I rushed my friend/attacker before he could reset himself and swing again.

We ended up on the floor with me on top. I was never really worried about being able to handle Victor. He was never a very imposing figure of a man; I'd determined that the night we met. That's another thing about the friendships we develop in this life. We size them up for their potential to bring us harm. No doubt Victor had taken my measure and decided I could probably take him in unarmed combat, which is why he wasn't unarmed.

Apparently Redman heard the commotion upstairs because

within a few minutes he appeared to break us up. He ordered the overcome Victor to leave the basement while he spoke with me. I remember echoing the command, adding that if Victor returned again I would kill him.

The fact that I don't remember what Red and I talked about after Victor left doesn't prove it wasn't important. I busied myself with fluctuating rage and with assessing the damage my TV suffered in the fracas.

What I do remember—what I'll never forget are the eerie sounds, wailing noises filtering down into my sleep early the next morning. A nameless dread crawled over me. I don't know why, but I knew exactly what the noises were about—and I knew who they were about.

I got out of bed and crept slowly up the stairs. A female voice repeatedly crying, "Oh my God! Oh my God!" grew clearer as I approached the door to the kitchen. Holding my breath, I pressed it open a crack and peered through.

Red was on his knees with his back to me. He was crying into his cell phone, "I'm tellin' you, man, your brother's dead! Dead with a needle stickin' outta his arm!"

Lying on the floor, his lifeless head resting in the crook of Red's free arm was Victor. I couldn't see his face from where I stood but I could see his right arm, could see the needle protruding from it just as Red had said. Standing off to the side near the door to the backyard was Clarice: young, pretty, fairly new to the game. Not an addict yet, but on her way. She stood frozen, both hands to her cheeks, eyes about to pop from their sockets, calling on God as she struggled to process the horror before her.

Welcome to the wonderful world of junkies, kid.

Suddenly I recalled the last thing I'd said to Victor and a crazy fear came over me. I didn't remember that we were friends, forgot that we had hustled together, gotten high together, even laughed together. It didn't occur to me that we'd tussled over something insanely petty and that we'd never have a chance to reconcile. Standing at the top of my "bedroom" stairs and peeking out at the fatal scene like some sort of spy, I could only remember my last words to Victor: *Come back down here and I'll kill you!*

The authorities would be here soon. It occurred to me that I didn't want to be present for that.

Self-preservation kicked in. Quietly I opened the door further, slipped past the weeping Redman without his noticing and left the building.

CHAPTER FOURTEEN

Redman got the call. The police wanted four of us from the house to report to the Clinton Avenue precinct house for questioning in the death of Victor Ramos—more than two weeks after Victor died.

The only surprise to me was that the "investigation" got as far as us. The realized mortality of a junkie via drugs is an occurrence that generates little passion and as little effort with the police. I suspect we were summoned only because someone needed to complete his paperwork and close the book on Victor.

Red, along with his wife, Vicki, Clarice, the wailing witness from that morning, and I rode together in Clarice's car. As I said, Clarice was not long enough in the game to have surrendered personal treasures such as her car and her driver's license to the gods of addiction. At this stage, she's nowhere close to believing she's an addict, but she'll get there. In a staggeringly short span of time, she'll be introduced to a side of herself she never imagined existed, a desperate and pathetic husk of her current pretty self, willing to do whatever it takes to secure her next hit. How else could she end up, riding with this crowd?

We rode in silence. We didn't rehearse what we'd say to the cops or even speculate on the questions they were liable to ask. We made no attempt to get our stories straight. I was sure the police knew about my fight with Victor the night before he died; everyone else did. I had no doubt that someone—for whatever favor he hoped to earn or just because he had a big mouth—had informed the authorities of every detail of our confrontation, right down to my threat to kill Victor. I knew that's why I made the guest list.

I felt a little apprehensive but not especially worried. After all, Victor had overdosed; everybody knew that as well. He'd injected a particularly potent dose of heroin with the street name, Sudden Death. There may have been a time when Victor could have handled so strong a shot, but with his liver ravaged and immune system severely compromised by hep C, Victor hadn't stood a fighting chance. I also knew the sordid tale of how and where he got the heroin, facts I was pretty sure the cops didn't have.

We didn't have to wait long after we arrived at police HQ. The detective assigned to the case, a familiar-looking guy named Barnes, was already waiting and called us into his office one at a time starting with Red, then Vicki, and then Clarice, whose interview was no doubt peppered with "What's a nice girl like you …" rhetoric.

My interview took longer than I expected. I thought the detective would get right to my fight with Victor and the threat I made afterward, but he seemed more interested in Victor's background: where he was from, if he had family, children. I answered as best I knew: I think Victor once said he was from Plainfield; yes, he has a brother, I think, but I never met him; maybe a daughter somewhere. I had begun to think maybe the detective didn't know about my fight with Victor until he brought it up just as I thought the interview was over.

Cops!

Yes, I responded after an interminable and awkward silence, Victor and I had fought, but it was really nothing. Neither of us got hurt or anything. *Why?* Well, he said I owed him money, but I didn't. Yes, I threatened him, but it was just talk, didn't mean anything. We fought all the time, I lied, but that's just how we got along. We were friends …

Except I didn't know him.

And then the four of us were returning to our drug-den-shooting-gallery-crackhouse home in Clarice's Ford Focus. I sat in the back with Vicki, barely aware we were moving. Barnes's questions kept bouncing back at me, reminding me that Victor wasn't born fully grown and addicted; he'd been young once, a boy like any other. He'd had a mom and a dad and played ball and gone to school. He'd despised and then liked girls, had aspirations, dreams.

But what did I know? I had sat in Detective Barnes office claiming Victor was my friend, yet I knew nothing about him, nothing at all.

I didn't attend Victor's funeral. I don't know when or where it was held. I don't know where they buried him. I was busy that day.

All that came to me during the ride home. I didn't even know where Victor was buried.

For the first time in a long time, I felt myself crying. Vicki noticed and called the others' attention to me. I pretended not to notice them noticing me.

"You okay, man?" Red asked and before I could reply, Clarice answered for me in all her new-to-the-game wisdom.

"He feels bad 'cause he never got to peace it out with Victor."

I said nothing, letting that explanation reign unchallenged. It was accurate enough as far as I was concerned, far more explanation than any of them had coming.

I didn't know Victor, didn't know anything about him. I didn't know where he grew up or if he ever married. I assumed he was about my age—but I didn't know. It never occurred to me to ask if he voted Democrat or Republican, if he was Baptist or Pentecostal. Before his death I didn't even know his last name was Ramos. I didn't know anything.

I knew he smoked Newport 100s when he could choose, drank any beer offered but preferred Colt 45, and like the female pop group, En Vogue. He smoked crack cocaine, was grateful to fill his hypo with the powder form I used when I had it to share, and his main love, his drug of choice, was heroin. Often on days when I was getting my unemployment, we'd sit down in my basement spot—he with his love and me with mine—talking about prosperity and success. Just two skinny, burnt-out junkies fantasizing about a life as far above us as the North Star is above the earth.

So if an association based almost solely upon mutual wretchedness and self-destruction may be considered friendship, Victor and I were friends. We spent time together, hustled together, bought and sold drugs together, watched out for each other—more or less—on the street and bad-mouthed the rest of the world (especially the other inhabitants in our building) together.

Yes, and we held out on each other. We cheated each other. It's the way the game is played. But we were friends, not a good or healthy or productive fellowship but it was what it was, what the gods of addiction allowed.

I guess even evil gods recognize and accommodate the human spirit's need for companionship. I remember from church that the first time God said something was not good was when He was commenting on man's aloneness. I suppose even in our lowliness— perhaps especially in our lowliness—we require the company of that kindred spirit, someone to join us in our wretchedness, to descend with us into that pit my former probation officer tried so valiantly to prevent my descent into.

And the gods? They do what they do. They twist, debase, and pervert every aspect of human experience, including friendship. They have the power to warp what I think, say, and do to their service—but my feelings are mine, intact and unalterable, demanding to be considered.   In other words, these gods who take everything have to give me *something*, even if only a junkie buddy, a fellow loser to be miserable with.

And now he was gone.

We were friends, Victor and me. I sat on the perfectly good mattress I'd found in my $150-a-month basement pad and thought about how much I'd miss Victor Ramos. I lit a cigarette and recalled the one time Victor and I had talked about God. Sure, we were both believers, never voicing negative or derogative views about Him (a common thread in our individual upbringings was that you don't speak ill of the Lord).

We talked about meeting God. We talked about being with Him in Heaven. We never considered the idea that we wouldn't go. After all, we were only playing the hands life had dealt us, doing what we had to do.

No sin in that, is there?

Clarice was right. I wish I'd been able to patch up my dispute with Victor, wish we'd had the chance to peace it out. In the days immediately following his death, I'd made somewhat a name for myself. In this game it doesn't hurt to be known for having disarmed and subdued one's attacker. I'd been strategically evasive when asked by visitors to the house about my fight with Victor, responding with feigned embarrassment to the congratulatory banter. There was a part of me, though, that enjoyed the notoriety, liked it that people knew I could be a formidable opponent if I had to be. I had cashed in on my fight with Victor, bought myself a bit of a reputation with his death—and we were friends.

A shaft of light sliced into my subterranean abode, signaling the sun's descent into evening. I rose from my bed and made for the stairs, the night's agenda already mapping itself in my mind. I wouldn't think about Victor again except in the odd, fleeting recollection.

I was alone again. Alone to get my hustle on, feed my addiction, and appease my gods. Victor was no longer burdened with such concerns.

Victor had stopped.

CHAPTER FIFTEEN

Dean and I were never really friends.

I remember Dean from the old neighborhood. He grew up around the corner from me on Princeton Avenue. I was in and out of high school when we became acquainted. In those days marijuana was the predominant drug of choice, and we kids smoked it incessantly. The house party was still the most popular venue for social interaction, although the club scene (called discos then) was coming on strong.

Dean's parents' house was the site of more parties than any other house I can remember. I'd gone to many but don't recall ever meeting his mom or dad. Just entering through the front door meant walking through a smoke cloud so thick I was already buzzing before even touching a joint. I don't know where Dean or his brother, Stephen, purchased such potent weed. He'd respond to our queries with impressive-sounding brand names like "Acapulco gold" and "Jamaican red," a prideful grin on his face and a cigar-sized blunt in his grasp. I was not a weed connoisseur and didn't know one brand from another, but I knew that if I wanted my money's worth with a pot purchase, Dean was the go-to guy. His talent for locating the best weed would translate into other areas of drug culture, however, and his recklessness in the lifestyle would eventually cost Dean everything.

I liked Dean well enough, I guess, but as I said, we never really made it as friends. We celebrated our birthday on the same day, though I'm not sure which of us was older—probably me by a year or two. I never saw Dean when he wasn't partying. I don't know if he finished school or went at all, for that matter. I don't know if he ever worked at a regular job. I found him just a little slick, conniving, and not especially trustworthy. In other words born—or at least made—for this life.

One day, Pete, another friend from the heydays of my youth took exception to Dean's slickness. I never got the full story but suspect Dean probably cheated Pete in some narcotics transaction. It ended with Pete giving Dean a most noteworthy thrashing (that's the way it was back then: few stabbings, fewer shootings, but many beatings). I last saw Dean maybe a year or two before I was sent to Rahway in '85. We wouldn't meet again until Dean came to take up residence in one of the second-floor rooms at the Passaic Street boardinghouse.

Dean had never been much to look at. Now he was less so: emaciated and pale, his eyes ringed and lightless. He moved slowly now and grinned a lot though he rarely laughed. I remember when he laughed all the time.

He rarely left the building except to get food or smokes from the bodega next door. He sold heroin out of his bedroom, and I'd dare to guess he injected as much as he sold. He shot dope all day, in fact—not that it mattered, not that he had anything else to do. Actually, Dean didn't have much of anything anymore except declining health and a dissipating life.

Dean was stricken with full-blown AIDS. He was an ice cube in the sun. The Passaic Street house was the last place where he would ever live.

Dean would be the next one to stop.

CHAPTER SIXTEEN

In the interests of continuity, you should know that Victor was alive when Dean moved in. You could even argue that Victor might still be alive if Dean *hadn't* moved in.

This is what happened: after Victor and I mixed it up in my place, Victor went up, dispatched by Redman and with my curses trailing after him, to the first-floor dining room. This was a beautiful home once. Solid mahogany everywhere, arched entryways, parquet floors—all fallen prey to the ravages of time and neglect. The dining room—obviously built with formal entertaining in mind—displayed a raised fireplace with hand-carved mantel and trim, a rusting, brass chandelier hung from a high, beamed ceiling. This had been a home in which the original owner undoubtedly had taken great pride; now crackheads sat at the chipped and scarred mahogany table, measuring and selling hits or filling and lighting their glass pipes. Dean had been living there several months by the time Victor and I had our altercation. He could usually be found in his room, smoking crack or nodding off his last fix, or both. Dean hadn't much energy for the streets anymore. Like I told you, he was an ice cube in the sun.

Sometimes Dean would put himself so far in the stratosphere, he became easy pickings for scavengers. For the most part Red saw to it no one molested him—save for Red himself, of course. I saw Vonnette fish through Dean's pockets more than once while Dean was too far gone to know, with Leon standing by as lookout, his menacing glare on me as I passed by. I really couldn't stand those two, a couple of vultures waiting for someone to drop. As for me, I didn't do crack or heroin so there was never anything of interest to me with that bunch. Dean's chief source of income was the disability insurance he received from social security due to his condition. He was as popular in that house when the mail ran once a month as I was twice a month with my unemployment income, and because he supplemented his SSD allotments with heroin sales, there were always a flock of predators circling around the slowly fading Dean.

There were almost no visitors in the dining room the night Victor and I fought, only Vonnette, Leon, Red, and Vicki and the ever-in-orbit Dean. It could be that Dean nodded off with his stash lying right there on the table, the proverbial sitting duck. Neither Vicki nor Vonnette used heroin, but chances are Dean also had the cash he'd made from that night's sales, crack money for the female crackheads. Red and Leon, hardcore bangers, of course would have helped themselves to whatever skag Dean possessed; skag with the ominous street name *Sudden Death*, as I later learned.

After Red broke up my fight with Victor, the latter went up to the dining room where he found the others. Dean, long relieved of his resources, was still out of it, and while the women smoked up his money, Leon was busy preparing injections of the opiate for Red and himself. I don't imagine he had a problem sharing with the angry and defeated Victor; there had been plenty, after all, it was free, and most significantly, the others now had a fall guy, someone to pin the theft on when Dean came around demanding to know what happened to his property.

Of course, blaming Victor solely for the rip-off was that much easier when Victor turned up dead. I didn't hear any of them accuse him to Dean; I didn't have to. I knew that bunch—so did Dean—but if he suspected anything beyond the witness the others bore against Victor, he said nothing. He had to live in that house, after all, and Victor wasn't around to refute the claims against him. But I think he knew. He knew and chose to believe the accusers.

And so Victor Ramos died, a high-potency grade of heroin known as Sudden Death coursing through his system.

Once when Red told me about that last shot Victor took, he tried to put across the impression that Victor had purposely overdosed. I don't remember his exact words—something about Victor telling him how much he hated his life in this world and how he hoped he'd be forgiven in the next.

He actually told me Victor said that. I only nodded, pretending to believe him, but I didn't and I always held it against Red that he would say it. Like the rest of us, Red was a liar and a thief. The electricity that powered the house Red acquired by shimmying up the pole out front and tapping into the source after the power company shut it off for nonpayment. He went down in the ground and turned on the water when that service was terminated, and he bribed the cable guy. I can't deny Red was cunning and resourceful; he was also undeniably a snake. He passed himself off as a stand-up guy, and I suppose to some he was, but not to me. I could never bring myself to dislike Red, but I didn't like him either. I let him invite himself to share my cocaine countless times, hoping he'd remember my generosity when times got hard for me and I couldn't make the rent. But I knew better. I knew that when the time came that I couldn't pony up, I'd be out on the street.

In addition to collecting Social Security, Dean had been appointed to some medical program that supplied him with 100 mg morphine patches, I assume to counteract pain of withdrawal from heroin. Someone obviously was under the impression that

Dean was detoxing. Sometimes he did use the patches, but mostly he sold them and invested his proceeds in heroin.

Dean came down to my place once. There were about six of us doing one form of drug or another. After they all left, I found a packet of four patches, apparently left inadvertently by Dean. I stashed them immediately to sell for cocaine later on.

After a while Dean returned, looking for his lost patches. I told him I didn't see them and asked if he was certain he'd lost them here. Of course he did, Dean insisted. He had them when he came downstairs and hadn't been anywhere else. I feigned offense and reminded him there were others down here at that time, any one of whom could have found his property. Dean got angry and called me a poor host and said that I was supposed to watch out for my guests and not let them get ripped off. Then I got angry. If I had known he had the patches, I told him, I could have looked out for him. He should have given them to me for safekeeping or at least let me know they were in his possession—and besides, I said, I wasn't sure he even had them down here.

Fuming, Dean left. That wasn't the last time we spoke, but it was the last time he came down to my place. I didn't care. We were never really friends anyway.

One night I found a bag of heroin on the street. I happened to be walking by when the woman dropped it while fishing for money out of her jeans pocket. When she walked off, unaware she'd dropped the package, I snatched it right up. As it was, I was on my way back to my place; a newly purchased gram of coke in my possession at the conclusion of a fair night's hustling. My first thought when I saw the bag drop was to inform the girl of her mistake. Occasionally I was given to such demonstrations of integrity, but tonight was not such an occasion. I took the skag home and gave it to Dean. He was in between checks at the time, hadn't a dime to his name, and had been suffering withdrawal all day. He looked at me with something akin to hero worship when I handed him that bag. I went down to my place feeling pretty good about myself, feeling as though I'd made up for my offense against him.

Dean's death was not as dramatic as Victor's. I wasn't around at the time. As it was told to me, Dean complained he was feeling "funny" and took a taxi to the hospital. I guess he knew.

None of us at the house saw Dean again. On a chilly, overcast day in October 2003, Dean Frederick Collins died. I had known Dean more than twenty years, yet we were never really friends. We grew up just blocks away from each other, were both born on December 3, and worshipped the same gods. We were never really friends but it didn't matter—not anymore. The ruthless and heartless gods that took Victor had now claimed Dean. I knew one day they would claim me as well and that wouldn't matter either.

But that minor tragedy was a concern for another day. For today I was still in the game. Dean was not. Dean had stopped.

CHAPTER SEVENTEEN

It is my belief that the gods of addiction would prefer to remain unseen and unknown, buried and hidden beneath the clutter of faults, frailties, and failings piled inside my broken soul like the rubble of a demolished building. I believe their anonymity makes them more effective destroyers, their role in my destruction continuing unchallenged and unchecked.

But every now and then the rubble shifts, the disorder is disturbed, an attribute or idiosyncrasy slips like a loose slat on a window shutter, and for the briefest instant I get a glimpse inside...

And I can see them. Evil glinting in the silver slits of their eyes, serrated fangs protruding from gaping black maws dripping venom, the remains of some unspeakable mauled thing clinging to their reaching, raking claws. And they have horns. Evil gods always have horns.

I can smell them. Their odor is ancient and deplorable, the smell of death.

And I can hear them. Conversing with each other in some loathsome, guttural dialect, a foul and profane language, unfit to hear, let alone understand. But I do understand—well enough to know they're talking about me and talking to me…

Demanding tribute. Demanding worship.

Then the memories come. Sometimes after I see them and I'm between highs—not sober—they make me remember.

It's cruel. They come unasked and unwanted, the memories flooding my consciousness and tearing at my conscience…

I'm a husband. I'm a loving stepfather. I'm a pillar of the community. I'm a faithful lover and generous provider to the woman I married. I'm a role model, a hero to her sons. They all regard me with pride and awe, gladly and gratefully professing me as their blessing from heaven and gift from God…

I'm a counselor, a leader of the lost to the light. I've earned titles and degrees; my name adorns the cover of highly regarded recovery texts and rehab formats. Hardened criminals seek and respect my counsel. They claim me as the heart of their inspiration, what they hope to achieve, to be…

I'm a United States Marine, the best of the best. Strong and valiant, heroic and brave. Only seventeen and as invincible as Superman. *Semper Fi…*

I'm a talented artist, a gifted speaker, and writer. The world stretches out at my feet. Barely out of high school and my future is nova-bright. The apple of my mother's eye and my father's pride. The wise and fearless first of ten…

I remember and the memories are altered, embellished, perhaps, but not exaggerated, presented to me not as the lie that was but the truth that might have been. The gods rub my nose in my unrealized potential and undeveloped ability in malicious mockery of what I became—their response to my having dared to see them.

It makes sense. What fun is there in even being a god if you can't occasionally flaunt your sovereignty, boast your influence, and bask in your authority over the lives of your worshippers?

They set all that is good and pure in me to rot and ruin, promoting only that which is base and wretched. They are exalted by my lowliness, empowered by my pain. From the moment I awake until the second I go to sleep I exist only to serve them.

We all do. I'm walking up Hanover Street just having crossed the bridge coming from Morrisville. Cigarettes are cheaper in Pennsylvania. I strolled over to buy several packs with the intention of selling "loosies" at a dollar apiece after the stores close.

I'm passing through an area of town notorious for its drug culture. There is no form or brand of controlled substance that can't be purchased in the four blocks I now traverse. It's a little past noon and the place is abuzz with activity, all drug related. In the tiny square of green that was intended for a park but ended up a junkie hangout, I see Lorie. I remember her from my days in junior high. She was gorgeous, popular, way out of my league. Today you can hardly tell she's even female: figure shriveled, face dark and sunken, eyes red and bulging. Her smile—given it may be interpreted as a smile—reveals fewer teeth than can be counted on one hand, and those are loose and discolored. Her hands are scarred and swollen from countless injections as though they'd been attached to an air hose and inflated. Her clothes are fairly clean but loose-fitting, baggy. And she has an odor. She was one of the prettiest girls from my childhood, a "fox" as we used to call them. She was bright and happy, a little stuck-up but so what? All the pretty girls from my childhood were stuck-up.

Today there's nothing Lorie wouldn't do, no demand too base or demeaning to discourage her acquiring her next hit. Nothing at all.

I see Marv coming out of the liquor store across the street. He's clutching the bag containing his purchase as though his life was in there. I suppose maybe it is. Marv is at least ten years my senior. I was in eighth grade when Marv's parents were killed in a car accident, leaving Marv and his older sister, Kathy, what folks in my area considered an enviable insurance inheritance, sizable enough to buy both children new cars, to begin with.

Marv was nineteen, tall, lean, and very good-looking, a college student when tragedy struck. His pursuit of higher education was the first casualty of Marv's grief; the new car one of the last. Over the years I saw from afar his decline into addiction. I swear he seemed to grow shorter.

And he became violent. Once smiling and gentle, Marv incorporated mayhem into his life as naturally as a maturing male incorporates a mustache into his appearance. It's like that with some of us: bloodshed practically becomes a means of communication, the solution to every problem, the answer to every question. I once saw Marv and a cohort beat up a kid while robbing him for his bicycle, beat him so badly I had to turn away, fearing I was watching a murder in progress. Unlike many of my peers, I just never developed the stomach for carnage.

When we were younger, and before his parents died, Marv treated me and Cookie, my best friend in those days, to ice cream. He asked us about our goals in life, encouraging us to be good, stay in school, and be obedient to our parents. With chocolate crust from our sugar-cone Drumsticks clinging to our lips, Cookie and I promised our benefactor we would. Marv smiled and rubbed our heads, a gesture Cookie and I didn't greatly appreciate, as I recall, but for the ice cream we were willing to suffer the indignity.

Marv wouldn't remember that day if I asked him about it now. He wouldn't remember buying me ice cream or giving me big-brotherly advice; he wouldn't remember me at all. He would simply size me up as a potential source of revenue and God help me if he decided I had anything of value in my possession.

I didn't know Kevin and Simmie from before. For all I know they were always the scheming, sorry pieces of work they are now.

Most of the day they're in another part of town selling placebos as the real thing and then returning here with their defrauded profits to score for themselves. They're a couple of rodents, crawling into house or apartment windows and making off with anything they can carry and sell, from the living room TV to the food in the cupboards. They get caught fairly often, by both people to whom they sold fake drugs and those whose homes they burgled. Sometimes a severe beat-down is the required fee for getting caught either during or after their acts, but not severe enough to make them consider a different vocation. They're a couple of punks whose association is built solely on their mutual cowardice and don't surmise that anything remotely resembling loyalty exists in their constant togetherness. They'd sell each other out in a heartbeat for pocket change.

We're a damaged brotherhood, a sick and sorry fellowship in this mecca of depravity. Strangers to one another and strangers to ourselves. Caught up in a life we would not have in our most twisted imaginings foreseen; involved in activities we would not have believed. We come from all walks of life and arrived by way of diverse circumstances, from innocent indulgence to soul-shattering tragedy, but however special or unique we were before, we're all the same here. We're nobody and nothing. We exist day-to-day with but one purpose: to serve the gods of addiction.

We are the worshippers: vigilant, dedicated, and devout. Our devotion to our gods has brought us together in this place. There are thousands of places like this place, all populated with us, the condemned, the damned, the addicted. No religion, sect, or cult can boast a more loyal following; no organization has enjoyed a greater increase. We pour ourselves into our faith, giving all we have and don't have to our insatiable and ravenous masters. They despise us; we don't care. They demean, debase, and abuse us; we don't mind. They suspend us above a cold, black eternity, demanding tribute; we eagerly oblige, surrendering our wills, reputations, talents, homes, families, and our lives. Nothing they require is too outrageous to gain our compliance; no demand above us, no transgression beneath us.

We burn all hope in the fires of our addiction, their altar of sacrifice. The flames rage hungrily and incessantly. We feed them tirelessly, shunning sleep and forsaking food. Our own comfort is inconsequential, our health irrelevant. We'll exploit our parents' forgiveness and abuse our children's hopes. We'll cheat anyone and steal anything. We are not to be trusted or believed: if our lips are moving we're lying. We know no restraint. We recognize no shame.

We worship our gods daily, every minute of every hour. They are greedy, selfish deities commanding all our energies and all our time; and so they get it. We will not fail to bring every offering, large or small, to immolate at their altar of sacrifice. We won't stop to rest, think, or dream. Neither hospitalization nor incarceration will deter us. Only death will bring an end to our worship. Only hell will outrage the flames of our devotion.

They are the sovereign gods of addiction—masters of our lives. We will entertain notions of abandoning them and may even succeed for a long time. But it's a supervised sobriety, recovery overshadowed by the specter of relapse. In the end we belong to them and they know it.

The first step in recovery is that "we admitted we were powerless over our addiction and our lives had become unmanageable." This is the most significant and abiding truth of our existence. We accept its reality knowing that our attempts to achieve recovery are at best a pathetic plea for "manageability": a petty ambition, a mundane goal. The gods mock it for a pointless endeavor, the remainder of our lives in privation, frustration, and misery and for what? *Manageability.*

And even if we are successful—if we can against all odds find and seize this elusive recovery—if we never return to that blazing altar of addiction again, it will be an achievement devoid of satisfaction. Our souls are forever scarred, our spirits damaged for all time just for having known them. We may acquire manageability, but we will never know victory.

I read somewhere that the most diabolical trick the devil ever played on mankind was to convince us that he doesn't exist. We, the addicted, through the bitter and tragic trial of our lives, can attest to this truth. How foolish we are, blind to the reality of spiritual dominance and demonic possession.

Earlier I said that the first best evidence of an evil presence within a person is the sudden and dramatic transformation of that person, the supernatural monstrosity it creates of its host. I believed that using a movie in which a young girl was made to float in midair, exhibit superhuman strength, and rotate her head 360 degrees served as a model.

But the gods of addiction are not so theatrical.

I look upon the gradual and sickening decay of a once-fox like Lorie...

A hostile and violent thug who once bought me ice cream...

Kevin and Simmie, scampering, skittering, and prison bound—if they're lucky...

Victor Ramos.

Dean Collins.

Countless others whose names I'll never know.

Me.

I see their faces and know their stories and the truth rings in my spirit with haunting clarity.

The gods of addiction don't create supernatural monstrosities...

They create natural ones.

CHAPTER EIGHTEEN

"What do you want, Mitchell?"

Well, the voice was unmistakably Mom's. If I had to, I could pinpoint her voice among thousands of screaming fans at Shea Stadium. Over the years, my ears have become acutely attuned to that voice, its every pitch, level, and inflection.

But tonight—or rather this morning—she sounded different. I'd never heard her this way. There was an uncharacteristic undertone I'd never encountered. I'd heard her angry, annoyed, exasperated, frustrated, and sorrowful. But this was none of those; this was something far worse. She sounded—for want of a better word—evil.

"Mom?" I said through my confusion. "Mom, it's me."

Of course it was me; she knew that. She'd ended that evil, un-Mom-sounding "What do you want?" with my name. It was after two in the morning, mid-February. An icy, stinging rain was falling and I was soaked to the skin. I'd never known a colder February. My fingers were numb and my feet were hurting, but not from the cold. The sores had come back. Actually, they hadn't stopped hurting that night they were treated—the night Chaplain Tommy visited me. They'd only felt better, less hurtful, than before. I'd been able to walk without wondering if the ground had sprouted nails. I could even run a little. I wouldn't win any marathons, but I could go from point A to point B more quickly than I had in a painfully long while.

Tonight, however, I was nothing short of miserable. My sneakers were wet and seemed to be shrinking, or maybe my feet were swelling, or maybe both. There was a solid knob of pain in my stomach too, and my head hurt. I was tired. I was hungry. I felt sick. I'd just made it this far from South Trenton where my efforts to hustle the night's fare had been defeated by the harsh weather. I knew I didn't have it in me to make it to make it to my place on Passaic—I doubt I could make it to the corner without collapsing.

"Can I come in, Mom?"

I hadn't been this way in a while, maybe twice in the last four months since Dean stopped. The first time was shortly after my interview with the police. I'd been feeling lonesome and sad. I guess that moment of emotional release in Clarice's car had put me in touch with feelings of homesickness. I went to my mother's house on Bond Street wanting nothing more than to be close with family. But it wasn't the reception I'd hoped for. Mom greeted me with barely a word, her face contorted with shock, while Brenda did absolutely nothing to conceal her disgust.

The funny thing about drug abuse is you don't really notice the effect it has on your appearance. Your aesthetic decline is gradual; you don't doubt you look bad but you're not fully aware *how* bad. At six feet even, my average weight is about 220 pounds. Now I barely moved the scale with the 165 pounds I dragged around. I could close my fingers around my arm as high up as my elbow, and my waist had wasted down from a size 38 to 32; I'd had to modify another belt with a nail in order to keep my trousers up.

But worst of all was my face: sunken cheeks and dull eyes, my skin ashen and powdery even when wet, what I now call the "shroud effect."

Natural monstrosities.

I hadn't meant to frighten or shock anybody. I didn't even want any money although I wouldn't have turned it down. I just wanted to come home, to be with family for a little while, to talk or even just sit, maybe have a bite to eat.

I just wanted to be among the living, but Brenda was having none of it. She started right in on me. Divorced herself, Brenda had moved in with Mom while she reassembled the components of her life. When she wasn't working or in school, she was on hand to "greet" me when I came around. I was never one for profanity, but Brenda had no qualms about expressing herself in cable TV language. What I hated most about Brenda was that she was in recovery. Her history of drug abuse was just that: history, close to fifteen years in the past. They say there's nothing more sanctimonious than a reformed sinner; in my sister's case, they were dead on. She behaved as though she'd never so much as taken a drink let alone had to deal with the streets for her next hit. She looked at me as though I were something vile and alien, cursing me for my lack of shame, accusing me of trying to kill Mom. Then she'd turn on Mom, admonishing her about helping me kill myself by supporting me in my "mess." After a bit, Mom agreed, telling me even as she fixed me a plate that she wouldn't have me at the house anymore. If I wasn't willing to get help, I could just get everything else from the streets I loved so much. I hated Brenda for that and called her self-righteous and hypocritical. I could never win in confrontations with Brenda. I had a gentle nature that—along with my guilty conscience—rendered me sorely disadvantaged in a verbal joust of insults and accusations while Brenda was not so restricted, going right for the throat. So I just shut down and suffered through her rant until I finished my meal and left.

The last time I went to the house was the day after my birthday. I deliberately chose a time of day when Brenda was at work, as I wasn't in the mood to go another twelve rounds with my younger sister. I was smiling and cheerful, thanking God for another birthday—such that it was.

Mom didn't share my mood. Her face—a face that lights up so beautifully when she's happy, may as well have been set in stone. She accused me of "playing" her (a Brenda word) and said she was tired. Tired of begging me to get help for myself; tired of being in conflict with the rest of the family for supporting me; and tired of watching me slowly kill myself. I didn't say anything as she withdrew cash from her purse and placed it in my hands. Then she looked straight into my eyes, her own brimming with utter sadness and told me not to come back to the house. She wouldn't let me in anymore. I accepted the money—of course—and she didn't pull back when I leaned close to kiss her. She didn't do anything.

Then I left and bought as much coke as I could purchase with the money Mom gave me.

"Mom?"

I don't know how long I'd been standing there. The winter rain seemed to have increased in intensity to a punishing downpour. The wool cap on my bald head was soaked and useless, as was the down-filled coat I wore. I couldn't stand much more of this. My feet were throbbing; in excruciating pain.

"You can't come in, Mitchell."

Can't come in? The words seemed obscenely unreal to me. Couldn't she see what was going on out here, that I was freezing to death in this weather?

"Momma?" Now it was *Momma.* As a boy, whenever I was hurt or scared or guilty, she was Momma. I bunched the folds of my coat in one ungloved fist and stood on tiptoe, trying to see inside the house through the drape-covered door window. The room beyond was dark. I couldn't even make out shapes. I could only sense movement by more than one. She wasn't alone.

"I told you, Mitchell, you can't come here no more. Go back where you came from."

It wasn't the first time Mom had spoken to me that way; she'd been annoyed, enraged, or outraged with me countless times in my life and countless more times in my addiction. This time though, there was something different in her voice, a note of cold, hard finality that I wouldn't have imagined my mother could possess, let alone convey. Confusion and denial collided in my belly; my throat hurt and the taste of bile filled my mouth. "Momma—Momma, I'm cold. Just let me in for a little while? Please?"

Nothing from the other side of the door. I could picture Brenda at Mom's side, bolstering her resolve, urging her not to give in. How I hated that meddling sister of mine.

"Go 'way, Mitchell. You ain't comin' in."

I just stood there, refusing to believe she could do this to me— me her firstborn.

"Momma—"

"Get off my porch, Mitchell."

"But...Mom—"

"I said go 'way!"

I could feel my heart skip a beat, and then it just seemed to stop altogether. It didn't seem possible. My mother had abandoned me, told me to go away and die. For the first time in my whole junkie life I felt truly, completely alone.

Tears of fear and rage stung my eyes. I held my trembling hands before me, watched them clench, dripping and frozen and powerless.

I wanted to die. I wanted to kill.

"So it's like that, now, huh, Mom?" I shouted at the closed

door. "I'm not your son anymore? You decided you don't love me anymore?"

And then I was running up Bond Street, shouting my anguish into the uncaring evening. My feet felt as though they'd been impaled with railroad spikes. I ran on them anyway, heading for my basement spot—the only home I had—assuming I wouldn't be refused admittance by Red. I hadn't given him money for rent in a while.

I had always been able to depend on Momma when I was feeling up against it; when my resources, options, and energy level had been reduced to zero. I could always go to Mom's to regroup, have a meal and a shower, score a few dollars, and occasionally bunk on her sofa for a night or two. And now her words, her tone, kept echoing in my head, attacking my heart like fists.

And I knew it was over. After putting up with a drug-addicted son for thirty years, my mother had finally learned to say no.

Crying, heartbroken, and completely alone, I ran blindly into the night, hating the mother who had rejected me and the sister who had poisoned her heart against me.

CHAPTER NINETEEN

I make this entry hesitantly and with great trepidation. I thought it over at length, prayed and meditated and prayed again, yet all my soul searching failed to help me conclude to any degree that afforded me even the smallest measure of certainty that I should do this: talk about her.

She's never been one to talk about her past, much less see it in print. Those of us who know her best and love her most have to confess to gaps in our knowledge about her adolescence and young adulthood. I must surmise she prefers it that way. I fear she may find her in-depth inclusion in this work a discomfiting challenge to her sense of privacy.

But I can't tell this story without her. Her presence in my life—the sorrowful witness she bore to the person I was and the inspiration she provided for the man I became—are second to only One other. Truly I would not have made it this far if not for her. To omit her from this telling would be to deny this story a truth so essential as to reduce it to a shallow work of fiction. And with that inescapable truth to encourage me, and despite my embarrassment for the informational gaps in my knowledge about her, I proceed, risking her disapproval and praying for her understanding.

I know she was raised in South Carolina. I know her mother

passed away when she was young and that she had a brother, Laphon, who disappeared, again while she was very young. Details of Laphon's fate remain sketchy even more than a half century later. At a time in this country when the inexplicable vanishing of a black man was a not uncommon occurrence, it was usually woefully sufficient to know that "white men got him." Such was pretty much the case with Private Casper Laphon Knowling, driven away in military police custody one day in 1945 and never seen again. She was about twelve at the time and he'd been her only sibling.

Sometimes—when I have the courage to think about it—I wonder at the enormity of the burden this unspeakable atrocity imposed upon her. I can't imagine the size of the sorrow, the depth of the loss, this impossible measure of grief and fear she'd be obliged to carry for all time.

I know that she was raised by her father and paternal grandmother. I know that she often stayed with relatives while Daddy Alonzo earned their living. What I don't know but extrapolated from the snatches of conversation I'd overhear between her and Brenda was that the hospitality of some of the aunts and cousins with whom she was entrusted left much to be desired. It wasn't that she was cruelly treated—at least not overtly—but not overwhelmingly adored. She ventured no explanations for the lack of civility demonstrated by her kin, but I knew. She was a beautiful girl with light-colored skin, long straight hair, and deep brown eyes left pretty much at the mercy of her dark and kinky "jigaboo" relatives.

I saw a picture of her once—a grainy, black-and-white photo that was old even as I studied it many years past. I instantly understood my father's attraction to her. I don't know if their romance was lengthy and formal or whirlwind (though I'm inclined to guess the latter). I am also unable to report the details of their wedding, civil or religious, sparsely or well attended, formal or casual. I vaguely recall seeing a photo of the two of them in wedding garb, but again, it was long ago and if said photo still even exists I wouldn't know where to begin to look.

I was born to them in 1955, and then came the twins, Brenda and Michael, followed by Val, Gail, Stephanie, Rodney, Albert (Fritz), Paul, and finally Peter. Dad worked hard to support us. I don't remember when he didn't have two jobs at a time. And there was rarely a time of want—for food or love—in our home. But while he had once been committed to winning her heart, Dad was not as dedicated to taming his own, to keeping it from wandering. For that they fought constantly. As I said, he wanted her because she was beautiful. Unfortunately, the world abounds with beautiful women.

I won't elaborate any further on that. I know she would not approve and would look upon it as disrespectful toward him. Anyway, such details are unimportant here, and for better or for worse he's still my dad.

Unhappiness is a contagious emotion. The absence of joy in a marriage is the absence of joy in a family. Sometimes it was all we kids could do to weather the storm of her outrage for his carnal trespasses, a storm that would rage and then calm only to rage again, continuing throughout my childhood with disconcerting regularity until finally in my sixteenth year, they were divorced. He'd been the love of her life. She would never devote herself so completely to another, and there were those who came to call, although—considering the size of the brood she managed, which included seven not-so-suitor-friendly sons—not many.

When I deem fit to abandon my self-centered concerns long enough to consider her, I marvel at her ability to endure, to keep going. But if it was an ability that came to her naturally, it was not one that sustained itself; it needed help.

She had begun to drink long before they separated. It was how she dealt with the void created by his suspicious and prolonged absences. After he left, her drinking increased. She grew morose and desolate, a perfect host for the soul destroyers. They moved in, filling her loneliness with their lying presence, imposing bitterness and anger upon her.

But somehow, she was able to free herself from her demons, abandoning them before their hold on her became unbreakable. Maybe it was the horror of seeing five of her ten children fall one by one under the destructive influence of substance abuse that restored her. She simply quit, cast them off before they could acquire godhood, cast them off and came to the aid of her afflicted offspring, praying and weeping and suffering for them through trial after trial. I was in prison by then; still she remained steadfast and sober. And she prayed...

...when her first daughter was taken into emergency, her life force slipping out through a near-fatal stab wound...

...when a police cruiser patrolling a back road in Lawrence Township—not on its regular route—spotted a car sinking in icy pond waters, her second son unconscious behind the wheel...

...when thugs targeted her third son—firing bullet after bullet into him—nearly crippling him—courtesy of a drug dealer with a grudge.

She stayed beside them and prayed for them and wept for them and asked God to spare them.

And God heard her prayers and He answered them. Her children survived to walk away from their demons.

In years to come—when my mood is pensive and dark—I would think about her—this woman I call "Momma" when I'm frightened, hurt, or guilty. I would think of her and I'd wonder if long ago—perhaps even before her parents were born—some cruel and heartless deal was made in heaven concerning her, a deal requiring her to know loss, loneliness, and suffering in catastrophic measure. I'd wonder if some insidious trade was struck: the survival of her children for the joy of her life.

And I'd consider this woman, "Momma," whose beauty time and trial had only been able to veil and not erase: her carriage a bit slower and heavier, yet her stature ever proud; her hair no longer black as a raven's wing, but an astonishing, lustrous silver-gray; and her eyes simultaneously bright and alert with timeless wisdom and unfathomably dark for all she's suffered. And I'd wonder: If such a callous deal had indeed been made, would she say we were worth it?

Was I worth it?

But those were musings for another time.

Tonight was the dead of winter and I was running in a relentless icy downpour. My clothing soaked, my feet throbbing with unspeakable pain, I ran from her house, crying my heartbreak into a dark and hostile atmosphere.

Crying my anger and pain against a woman who was guilty of nothing more than loving me enough to finally tell me no.

CHAPTER TWENTY

I should have known better.

Under normal circumstances (or what passes for "normal" in the daily routine of a junkie) I would have. But for the weeks following my rejection by Momma I'd been a man on a mission—except I didn't quite know what the mission was. Injecting cocaine until my arms were like pincushions was mission enough, I suppose.

My brain was on fire. I'd gone back to Bond Street twice since that night; Momma still wouldn't let me in. She wouldn't even open the door but only shouted from the other side of the barrier that I needed to seek help. Even without Brenda on hand to encourage her, she wouldn't budge. I was stymied. My last safety net in the world was gone; my final reserve exhausted.

Seek help—in other words, check into another program. But I was through with programs, through with professional addicts lording over me that I was amateur, through with meetings and institutional formats geared to reinforce the truth of my wretchedness. I didn't want to hear from another program. I said as much to Mom, and that pretty much terminated the conversation. She ordered me off her porch again, refusing to let me in for so much as a drink of water.

With the thought of my mother abandoning me renewing itself

in my mind by the hour, I grew wild and reckless with self-pity. I started "visiting" the shopping centers with an increased regularity that should have raised the suspicion of even the dullest clerk or security guard. Disregarding style and finesse, I stole with an abandon that may have convinced an observer (or therapist) that I was trying to get caught. I was not. I was trying to get high—trying to *stay* high.

Earlier I talked about an attitude of selfishness as a tool of recovery and its harmful effect on my marriage. I have to confess now in all fairness that the idea of the selfish pursuit of recovery is not completely without merit. In objective therapeutic reasoning, it simply implies that the addict should be as dedicated to staying sober as he'd been to getting high. From that standpoint alone I couldn't be more in agreement because addiction is first and foremost a selfish existence. No conviction, responsibility, or obligation even approaches addiction in terms of priority. Addiction is not frightened away by the law or shamed away by moral code; it is not explained away by psychology, treated away by medical science, or driven away by social order. No person, however intimate his or her relation to the addict, can stand in the way of his single-minded devotion to his "disease."

Addiction is first and foremost selfish and secondly self-destructive, overriding its host's concern for even his most basic personal requirements, such as nutrition, health, and hygiene. The average junkie suffers a number of health issues from rotting teeth to malfunctioning internal organs. He is prone to all manner of respiratory distress. He is offensive to look at, to listen to, to smell.

Lastly, beyond self-destructive, addiction is suicidal. In many rehabs addiction is rightly referred to as "committing suicide on the installment plan." Junkies take insane risks in pursuit of their next fix, violating the cardinal rules of self-preservation. They cheat and steal wantonly, often victimizing people who know who they are and where to find them. They attempt strong-arm robberies against uncooperative would-be marks of superior strength and stature when they themselves are too emaciated to provide a respectable challenge and too debilitated even to escape. They get mauled by guard dogs while burglarizing businesses, shot by residents they'd foolishly gambled would not be home. In drug-induced stupidity they attempt to sell stolen merchandise back to the original owner and get beaten to within an inch of their lives.

All of this does not even take into account the Russian roulette practice of using drugs to begin with. Junkies share needles, often taking only superficial—if any—precautionary measures, regularly risking exposure to HIV and hepatitis C without an instant's hesitation. I once used a syringe I found in an abandoned building when the "tools" I brought with me jammed and I blessed my lucky stars. I have been shot, stabbed, and beaten to "within that inch" as I faithfully worshipped the gods of addiction.

Then there's the substance itself. Because the average junkie lacks a degree in chemical engineering, it's probably safe to say he doesn't know what he's introducing into his body. He purchases from his local dealer, taking on faith that what he's about to drink, swallow, smoke, snort, or inject has not been diluted with junk or enhanced with poison, "trusting" his purchase to take him to the brink of death without putting him over.

And that brings me back to this chapter's opening statement: I should have known better.

I'd been going all out for days on end, a man on a mission, as I said. Lost in self-pity, dejected, and angry, I set my mind to the only thing that mattered to me, the only thing I got out of bed for. I don't remember the last time I gave Redman money for rent. I'd stopped turning over even the ten or so dollars we agreed upon when my unemployment dried up. Every penny I hustled went into my arm.

Needless to say, Red took exception. The last time he came downstairs to ask me for money and saw me shooting up, he got angry. If I can buy that stuff, he argued, I can pay my rent. True enough—still it sounded almost ridiculously comical coming from him. I merely shrugged an uncaring "whatever" as he threatened me with eviction if I didn't come across soon.

I knew my residency at the Passaic Street house was near its end. I didn't feel about it one way or another and wasn't at all intimidated by the prospect of living on the street. Others managed, and so would I. Besides, I never really liked it there anyway. I didn't like the people who lived there or those who came and went all day long. It was never my home. People died in that house.

There was a rat in that house; a large, gray, shaggy-haired thing. Some nights when I was down there doing my junkie thing, I'd spy him scampering along the gray steel pipe that ran diagonally across the ceiling connecting the house plumbing to the sewer system—doing his rat thing. I never bothered to clock him, but I'd say about the same time—around midnight—he made his way (always heading in the same direction, from the back of the house toward the wall leading to the street), going about his vermin business. The pipe, his chosen means for travel, passed above the foot of my bed; he literally walked right above me, yet aimed not so much as a glance in my direction. He had his concerns; I had mine. This was his home, but it was never mine.

No, I didn't like this house. To my eyes neither Red nor any of the others were any different from that rat, no worse and certainly no better. I suppose I should have lumped myself in with the rest of them; I was the same as they. But it didn't matter. I felt that when Red tossed me—when he put me out of this repugnant hovel—I wouldn't care.

I went to Prospect Street to score. The trip had taken three times longer than normal because my feet were really hurting. The lighted OPEN sign on the door of the liquor store informed me that it was at least earlier than 10:00 p.m.—the store would be closed otherwise. I made a mental note to stop by for a bottle after concluding my business on the street.

It was unseasonably cold for March (it seemed to me it had been an unseasonably cold winter). I was wearing the down coat I wore that night on Momma's porch. It was a good coat, actually. I got it new at a Salvation Army coat giveaway in November. It provided fair protection from the cold, but it wasn't right for wet weather. It was dirty now, and I felt cold because I'd injected an inordinate amount of coke the past few days—a lot even for me. That means a lot of water was coursing through my veins, resulting in chills. My nervous system was running without a fly wheel. My heart was racing, and when I spoke, my words sounded broken and unintelligible even to me, a condition that coke users—powder snorters and mainliners and crackheads—refer to as "skeed" or "skeed up."

The street was bustling with activity, all manner of hustle going on. Male junkies were making purchases or sales, females were making purchases or sales or trying to barter sexual favors for drugs with males making purchases or sales.

I could usually find my connection at the first house on the street near a newly blacktopped alley. He or one of his cohorts would be on the porch. I don't know if any of them lived in the house; the prohibition against knocking on the door was widely understood. Directly across the street from there another alley— unpaved and litter-strewn—led around to an abandoned building where crackheads hung out drinking beer and smoking processed "rocks" of cocaine. When my guy or his partners weren't "home," they could often be found back there making sales. I felt a stab of annoyance as I approached the house and saw no sign of them. I thought about their alternative location, dreading the rocky ground on the tortured soles of my feet. Grudgingly I considered my very few options. Cocaine in powder form was not in huge demand in this area, therefore only a few dealers had it. Heroin and crack were the big sellers. I knew of one or two places nearby. One was rarely in supply and the other was often an unsatisfying score in terms of quality.

I stood bone-cold and trembling a few minutes more; thinking over my iffy alternatives while hoping my usual guys would materialize at their "appointed post." Another minute passed, and I turned to try one of the other spots, resigning myself to accept weak cocaine as better than no cocaine.

"Hey, baby boy!"

I stopped and turned toward the shout. Coming out of the alley across the street and heading my way was a local crackhead known as Scientific (don't ask me where he got the name), a virtual fixture in the area like a street sign or sewer grate.

"Hey, man, you lookin'?"

I regarded the lanky, bow-legged junkie with a wary eye. Guys like Scientific often earned "treats" from dealers by running sales, bringing them buyers. I didn't have a problem with that although I preferred not to deal with middlemen. But I was cold, really miserable now. I nodded toward my guy's house and then indicated the alley Scientific just exited. "They back there?"

Scientific replied, "Sold out 'bout a hour ago. They in the bars now, say they done for the night. But I got 'soft' if you lookin'." He held out his hand, and I regarded the glassine bag in his palm suspiciously. Heroin was sold in bags of this type, not cocaine, which Scientific had indicated with his use of the word "soft." My eyes met with his again and I shook my head.

"I don't do skag, man."

"No, baby boy," the skinny junkie grinned with his big yellow teeth. A lot of people in the area had taken to the expression "baby boy." I thought it sounded stupid. "This ain't 'P'; it's 'soft.' I just ain't have nothin' else to put it in."

I should have known better. Under normal circumstances, or what passes for "normal" in the life of a junkie, I would have. I would not have so much as engaged a player like Scientific in conversation about the weather, let alone a discourse in unorthodox drug packaging. I would have taken one look and told Scientific where he could put his glassine bag. But I'd been flying for days on end, shooting up coke like there was no tomorrow. My system was racing, my judgment fried. I was cold and miserable (*skeed*) and my feet were in hell.

I was running on autopilot as I paid Scientific and took the package. Despite every instinct screaming at me that I'd been played, I told myself it was a good buy; I'd gotten what I came for. That's the way it is after the deal is irreversibly done. All the way home you tell yourself it's okay.

It's okay...it's okay...

It was not okay.

The instant the last of my purchase was inside me, I knew I was in trouble. My vision blurred and my fingers went limp, letting the spent syringe drop to the dirty oval-shaped throw rug beside my bed. Its contents were now my contents, cutting a deadly swath through my system. I could almost hear my heartbeat and blood flow decelerate to a life-endangering crawl.

I had overdosed on heroin.

I was dying.

CHAPTER TWENTY-ONE

It was an honest-enough mistake. When I mixed the powder I bought from Scientific with water, it dissolved on contact—the way true cocaine does. Heroin, as I remembered it, required heat, the flame of a match or cigarette lighter to liquefy it to injection-capability. Since I didn't hang out with the skag crowd, however, I hadn't been on hand to receive updates regarding modern chemistry's advancements with opiates. My mixture also lacked the antiseptic alcohol aroma attributable to cocaine, but due to my agitated skeed condition I didn't even think to subject it to the smell test. When the powder melted down so obligingly, I believed it to be the real thing.

It was real, all right. Real poison. It was likely Scientific had found or stolen a bag of heroin and sold it to buy crack, his drug of choice—sold it to me under the fraudulent claim that it was my drug of choice.

I had used heroin once many years ago. I was with a few buddies (way back when I actually had buddies) in a drug den on Academy Street. I smoked pot while watching them prepare several doses (using *fire* to dissolve the stuff). Relatively new to intravenous drug use, I accepted a freely offered hit, mostly out of curiosity.

I regretted it right away. I felt drunk, clumsy. I staggered, sweating profusely, eyelids drooping, and vomited. Someone cursed. Someone else muttered something about me overdosing with the added command to "get him outta here." Two of them brought me outside and walked me around. I felt frightened and helpless. I couldn't wait for that "high" to pass. It seemed like an eternity before it finally did.

And I never touched the stuff again. It was a stupid, pointless high. In shooting galleries, they snort or mainline heroin and then just sit around nodding, drooling, scratching themselves, and looking like dead people.

It's dangerous stuff. People shoot heroin and die. They just nod their way into the grave. I've never known or even heard of anyone overdosing on cocaine. It's abuser-friendly. Safe.

I felt myself descending, lying down on the bed. I wasn't supposed to do that. I needed to get up, get up and walk, get my system in gear before I shut down—before I died.

I couldn't move. My limbs wouldn't obey my mental commands to push my body up to a standing—or even a crawling—position. There was a sound like the thunder of rushing water in my ears, and then there was nothing. I couldn't feel myself breathing. I couldn't feel anything at all except heat—feverish, hellish heat.

Panic crept over me. I rolled my eyes (I think), straining to focus. The basement ceiling loomed into view above me, a utilitarian mess of wiring, pipes, and wood floorboards appearing to rise as the rest of the room seemed to descend and fall away from the world.

Taking me with it.

I had overdosed. I was dying.

I thought to scream, to cry out for help. I don't know if I succeeded. I couldn't feel my mouth open to produce sound, couldn't feel my vocal cords respond to my desperate commands.

I'm dying. Oh, God...God...I'm dying.

For what seemed a long time I lay in the grip of mind-numbing fear and felt myself drifting down, down, deeper into death. Then inexplicably I drifted to a halt and simply existed, neither alive nor dead, floating in a cold and lightless void. I could taste and smell sweat, and I remembered that other time I overdosed, remembered throwing up. If it happened now with me flat on my back I'd gag, choke on it. Horror enveloped me as I thought of drowning—drowning in my own vomit. There were no buddies around to help me now. I was alone. Alone to produce my own flood—expel a sour, caustic flood from my guts and...and drown in it...

Help...help me, I'm dying.

With all the concentration my fading will could summon, I sent my silent cry into the house above me. Someone would be there—someone was always there—to hear my telepathic distress call and come down. I thought about Redman. I didn't see him when I came in, not that I was looking for him—looking *out* for him would be more the truth—but usually the dining room was full to capacity with "guests." If Red came down to hassle me for his overdue rent, I'd be saved ...

And probably evicted.

Red and I had never discussed how he explained Victor's overdose on his property to the police. I imagine the authorities had been curious, to say the least. Having to explain a second drug death—my death—not long after might prove embarrassing for poor old Red.

With that my thoughts drifted to my old buddy Victor, dead on the kitchen at the top of my "bedroom" stairs, dead in the room above me. For months after it happened, visiting junkies had referred to the scene of Victor's death as "Hell's Kitchen." A pall fell over me as I considered. If "hell" was a floor above me, then where was *I*? What's lower than hell?

My grim reverie came to an abrupt halt as activity within my dying form took my attention. I could feel—even hear—my bladder and bowels relax, vacating themselves. I was wet and dirty—even dirtier now. I shuddered internally with humiliation. This is the way they'll find me, I thought, just another junkie lying dead in his own filth.

And then—appropriately perhaps—I thought of *them.*

Thought of them and looked for them, searched my poisoned and ebbing essence for the spirits that had for so long occupied me like malevolent squatters, usurping my innocence, my goodness, my life. I sought out the gods to whom I had surrendered everything—*more* than everything. I screamed soundlessly for them to show themselves, to come out and see what they'd accomplished, to enjoy their handiwork.

I know you're here...know you're here...

I was almost desperate to see them again, desperate to find that veil behind which they hid and throw it aside. I wanted to look upon their evil, ugly forms and stand face-to-face with them before I died; before, like Victor and Dean and countless others, I stopped.

Come out, come out, wherever you aarrre...

Because I was alone. Alone and dying. Alone and soiled and helpless like an abandoned infant. Because I was afraid. Afraid to die alone. I looked for them because even the company of my tormentors, the witness of my destroyers, was preferable to dying alone.

Come on...

And they were all I had—all I had left. I had thrown away all I had—forsaken everyone I loved to serve them.

Come out...

Sacrificed love and family and future for them—all I was and could ever be—burned on their altar, offered in worship to them.

Please...

They owed me that much—that much at *least.*

Please...

But they would not answer, would not respond to my fading spirit's plaintive wail for their audience. At odd times in the past I could more than sense their presence, knowing even when I *didn't* know that they were watching me. Now when it mattered—when I wanted—I couldn't detect a hint of them, not so much as a shadow's footprint to prove their lying reality—their final insult to my own.

Something happened then, something that at least gave me a sense of the time.

Movement caught my eye. Movement along that pipe spanning the ceiling of my basement abode—my tomb.

At or around midnight he always made his way. His plump, shaggy, gray form scampered along with repulsive grace, going about his rat business. Heading toward the front of the house for his private exit into the night, with not even a glance in my direction—until that night.

He paused, stopped. His rodent feet clamped against the round surface of his bridge and he turned his rodent head. He looked at me, beady black eyes peering into mine as he assessed my predicament, my helplessness.

His nose twitched, gray whiskers feeling the air for danger—or opportunity. Rat lips drew away from rat incisors, baring rat fangs—and he grinned—or something.

Then he resumed his routine, returning to his nightly stroll of the outdoors. I watched, both horrified and awed as he acquired the far wall, squeezing his fat rodent's bulk through a hole less than half his size, his nasty pink rat's tail twitching after him.

He was gone, leaving me to wonder if—when his nocturnal agenda was completed—he would return. Would that—that natural monstrosity come back to do his rat's thing with *this* natural monstrosity? And with that miserable prospect to trail me into death, my thoughts went to the family that would inherit the mess in the basement of the Passaic Street dope house: the brothers and sisters for whom I had been an endless source of embarrassment and shame for so many years. I wondered how they'd take this sorry bit of news; how they'd react to hearing I'd been found this way.

What have I done?

And what about Momma? I thought about that cold, rainy night on her front porch, for the first time seeing through eyes that weren't glazed over with anger, self-pity, and cocaine. For the first time ever it occurred to me how hard it must have been for her to reject me, her firstborn. The concept of "tough love" is a difficult one for many to accept; it is usually a last-ditch effort by frustrated family members who had repeatedly tried every other means imaginable. For my mother it came after trying for three decades to reason, plead, shame, browbeat, wait, and pray her oldest child back to sanity.

Oh, God...God, what have I done?

How would she take this? Would she assume any responsibility, believe it came to this because she turned me away? What would that do to her?

I don't remember the last time I considered someone's feelings ahead of my own. Now I was filled with regret and shame for the misery and disgrace I'd brought upon those who loved me. As my mournful spirit slipped inexorably into the abyss, I could hear myself begging God to be with my family...

Please, God...please...

Begging Him to spare them the burden of this final indignity, this last disgraceful thing I did. Asking Him to strengthen my sister and brothers in their recovery; that they be made stronger by the sorry example I made of my life and that they never again succumb to the gods that took me.

That He would be there for my mother, to console and comfort, sustain and keep her. When all was said and done, I knew Momma loved me, that she would not take this well. I asked God to not let it break her.

I'm sorry...I'm sorry...

And then I asked Him to forgive me, to make them forgive me. I asked that someday... someday they might look back and remember me as a different person; a better person.

Forgive me...please...forgive me.

I could hear my breathing, shallow and weak. My surroundings lost their distinction, blending into shapes and fading to black. I wasn't not afraid anymore—not of dying or of being alone. I felt no fear at all, only a deep and abiding regret for the life I wasted and the people I hurt.

I lay still and uncomplaining as the darkness crept over me.

"It's all right, now, I have you."

The words, clear and strong, reached into the darkness and pulled me out. Though I'd never heard the voice before, I've never known a sound more familiar, more reassuring. My vision reversed from black to blurry. Objects reassumed shape and substance...

"Don't be afraid."

Suddenly I was fighting my way back through the darkness, straining toward the light. There was someone at my bedside speaking to me. I could feel a warm hand holding mine. The touch was comforting.

I attempted to turn my gaze upon my visitor, my rescuer. I still couldn't move. All my senses were returning, yet I still couldn't move. For the first time since this nightmare began, I thought about a hospital. I needed medical attention. I parted my parched lips to speak. Thank God, my voice—though dry and scratchy—returned.

"Help me..."

"Yes," my visitor responded. "Don't be afraid."

I'm not afraid, I wanted to say, but the words wouldn't come, perhaps because they weren't true. I was afraid, more afraid than I'd ever been, but not of dying. I was afraid because now I have a chance to live.

"Help me," I repeated. My voice was stronger, still dry and raspy, but improving.

"Yes, I'll help you."

My eyes filled with tears. I was still afraid, but the fear felt good, felt like life. I wouldn't die down here after all.

A wave of gratitude washed over me and with all the strength I could summon, I closed my fingers on the hand and with what strength I had left squeezed them in thanks.

Consciousness faded as the cool black abyss took me.

CHAPTER TWENTY-TWO

I am inclined to believe that the gods of addiction do not take special pleasure in their worshippers' deaths. While the declining mortality of those they defile may provide them with evil amusement, I'm convinced that they are more concerned with their survival than their host's destruction. Toward this end, therefore, I'd guess a living junkie would be far more useful than a dead one. A worshipper who has "stopped" can no longer bring tribute to their sacrificial altar, can he?

I think the gods didn't respond to my calls to appear to me as I lay dying because they weren't particularly pleased to see me die. Don't get me wrong, I know my death is their ultimate goal; I just think they'd be as content if that death didn't come for a very long time, so that I would remain in active addiction indefinitely.

I awoke, head throbbing, throat sore and dehydrated. The light, though dull, hurt my eyes. I stank of my own bodily excretions.

I lay still, recalling my ordeal. I had overdosed on heroin. I almost died. Alone in a drug-house basement, I almost died. Revulsion shuddered through me with the notion. With my most supreme effort, I pushed myself up and sat on the edge of the bed that had almost doubled as my cooling table. Slowly my head stopped reeling as a familiar taste—like a faithful old friend—spread over the surface of my tongue, bringing its associative craving to the forefront of my thinking:

I wanted cocaine.

The thought brought no shame with it. It's just the way it is: a junkie faced with his mortality may confess with the most righteous of saints, but if he's still standing when the smoke clears, he's still a junkie with masters to serve and gods to appease.

Yes, I know how despicable that is, but look, I was once shot by thugs intent on robbing me for my bicycle and the three rolled joints in my shirt pocket and stabbed over a craps game for winning—not cheating, but winning. I was beaten by more attackers than I could count until I could barely crawl, let alone walk away. I spent the night bound and gagged in the trunk of a stunning, baby-blue 1972 Buick Electra 225 while my kidnappers debated whether or not to kill me for the two ounces of coke I'd stolen from them. I went head-first through a plate glass window to escape capture by junkie twin brothers known to slit their victims' throats for pocket money. I managed to elude the psychopathic siblings, but the taxi that clipped me as I fled spun me like a top, nearly taking my arm off and those things are not only not all, they're not even the worst.

And this latest? This latest was a heroin overdose and not even my first. Add it to the list. Put it on the pile.

I wanted coke.

Of course I needed to get cleaned up first. I couldn't stand the smell of myself. The whole basement reeked of my excretions. I couldn't believe the stench hadn't drifted upstairs bringing someone down to complain.

But someone did come.

I got shakily to my feet, holding on to one of the basements support columns to steady myself. How long had I been down here like this? Stumbling once, I went to turn on the TV—no simple matter since my fight with Victor. The ON/OFF knob had been dislodged when he swung that pole at me. I achieved that function now by leaving the set on and unplugging it when I wanted to turn it off.

I felt board-stiff and could barely reach up without groaning when I plugged the power cord into the A/C adapter screwed into the ceiling light. The battered old set crackled and sparked to life. The sweaty, pious face of one of the numerous, nameless evangelists indicative of weekend programming filled the screen. I stared, mouth agape and unbelieving.

Sunday. It's Sunday.

Sunday!

Three days. I'd been down here—lying in my own urine and excrement, alien poison trying to kill me—*for three days.*

I trembled with the thought. Three days in this repugnant hole and no one had come down to ask for a cigarette or bug me for the rent or to see if I were breathing.

But someone did come…had spoken to me…held my hand

I fought to clear away the cobwebs and fog from my mind and remember my unknown visitor. No face, no image answered my search. I couldn't recall if the visitor were male or female, couldn't remember the voice except that it had been familiar—had taken away the fear of dying.

"It's all right…don't be afraid…I have you."

I have you. Such a strange thing to say to someone on the edge of death—just the right thing, I suppose, but strange nonetheless. Who had that person been? Why did he or she come to comfort me and then just leave me down here?

"I have you."

It occurred to me that my mysterious guest had been a hallucination, an apparition contrived by my short-circuiting, heroin-blasted brain.

"I have you."

It occurred to me—but you couldn't pay me to believe it. In the polluted well of my spirit I knew someone had come down and sat with me. Someone real, as real as the ordeal had been. As real as my impending demise had been. My visitor had been real.

I moved about in a daze, gathering together fresh (or fresh*er*) clothing and toiletries. I had to get out of the soiled things I was wearing. They felt like they were glued on. I needed a shower. I needed a shave. I needed to get out of this house, get some air, clear my head, get my hustle on, score some coke.

On the TV the portly preacher was blathering on about the creation of hell on earth.

No kidding, Rev! I can give you an exact address!

I mounted the stairs as quietly as I could. As long as neither Red nor anyone else had seen fit to look for me all weekend, I certainly didn't need them now. With a little luck, the whole house would be sleeping off last night. I could get in and out of the bathroom and then out of the house without drawing unwanted attention.

I arrived at the top of the stairs, reached for the door. And stopped.

The slide bolt was in place. The door was locked—locked from this side. I had locked it when I came in.

So how...?

How did my visitor gain access to the basement? How did he or she get in?

Dumbly I looked around, unsure what I was looking for. I knew the door to the kitchen was the only way in or out of the basement. The metal door leading from there to the backyard was chained shut to discourage burglaries, and there was only one street-level window—barred, also to thwart break-ins.

"It's all right..."

How...how did...

"...don't be afraid..."

...how did you get in?

"...I have you."

My heart began to pound, thudding in my chest, booming in my ears. I clutched the bundle of clothing and toiletries against my torso, as though trying to calm or at least muffle the noise of my cardiac overactivity before it woke someone.

Then came the memories, unbidden recollections of three horrifying days lying on that bed consumed with guilt and remorse and fear and death. For three days I'd been no more significant than a squashed bug on a basement floor, even the smell of my own death and decay unworthy of notice.

Tears stung my eyes, pouring out of me in an endless torrent. I sank to the floor, a weeping infant in a soiled diaper. Broken, ashamed, and frightened again, I lifted my head and cried my anguish into the dusty basement ceiling.

"Okay...okay, you say you got me, but I'm still here; still me; still a mess—so what am I s'posed to do? If you got me, what're you gonna do with me?"

No answer came. I didn't expect one; somewhere inside I'd hoped for it, but didn't expect it.

My nose ran; tears poured from me in a torrent and confused and angry, I wept.

"What'd you save me for anyway? Why'd you bring me back to this?"

CHAPTER TWENTY-THREE

I once said that junkies don't die, they stop, but that's not entirely true. They—we—don't always just stop. Dean Collins didn't stop. His death was gradual, a wasting away. He melted like an ice cube in the sun.

I'd forgotten I'd said that about him. Forgotten until I had come to realize that now I was like Dean: fading, dissolving, decreasing until finally I'll be gone.

I was an ice cube in the sun.

No answer came to me that Sunday morning; not while I waited and cried, nor while I bathed and cried, and not when I hit the streets to do my junkie thing.

I'm not sure what I wanted. Maybe some thunderous, celestial voice offering redemption for my troubled soul and direction for my wayward spirit?

To hear the voice of God, maybe. Speaking a clear and certain way out of that basement, out of that life. His assurance that I need not be afraid, that He had me and would deliver me to some place new and clean.

It seemed foolish to me now. I'd spent a great many years— thirty of them—debasing and defiling myself, devoting myself to declining virtue and deteriorating morality. Three decades to sabotaging personal success, eroding relationships, and alienating the law. I'd given my life to elevate demons to gods. Where else *would* I be than in a basement? Where else would I die?

Sometimes—when I wasn't running and entertained no standing aversion for self-evaluation—I'd look at myself and wonder what brought me to such a sorry state. What repressed traumatic event or circumstance was it that made me this—this self-destructive, self-loathing thing I am? Surely somewhere—in my childhood, in my infancy, in the womb—I became the victim of a crime so heinous the enormity of it had to be hidden away in my subconscious, there becoming the gateway to the destroyers of my soul. I wondered if, perhaps even before I was born, I'd been marked, claimed and set aside by some nameless, obscure evil. Can it be, I'd wonder, that I never had a chance? That I was meant to come to this?

In the beginning God created the heavens and the earth. Had He decided this for me even then?

But those are the bitter musings of every junkie seeking absolution for the wrong choices he made, justification for his warped and wicked life. Because when the last self-pitying lie has been told, all that remains is the glaring, cold, and inescapable truth: I'm here because I'm a loser, stupid and worthless, better off dead.

What made me think God would want to hear from me? Why would I believe He'd have something to say to me, anything to do with me?

I was homeless by the time the earth's revolution around the sun brought creation into the month of April. Redman had finally gotten around to giving me the boot, telling me he'd rented my in-arrears spot to someone who wanted to move in by the first of the month. There was little by way of argument I could offer and what's more, I just didn't care.

I didn't have much in terms of personal belongings as I packed to leave—or, I should say, not much left. I had accumulated a fairly decent wardrobe after my release from prison, including more than a dozen suits and ten pairs of dress shoes for church. Most of it was gone now, sold for drug money or gone to pot for lack of maintenance. It was still a fair amount of property for one who would be living on the street—a burden, really, to lug along with me everywhere I went. I decided to settle for what I could stuff into a backpack and leave the rest for Red to dispose of as he deemed appropriate. Not that he hadn't already helped himself to some of my best stuff anyway; he was the only other person in the house with a key to my place, and I wasn't so continuously blitzed that I didn't know I'd occasionally been "visited" in my absence.

And so I bid adieu to my Passaic Street residence without so much as a backward glance. I'd lived in that place more than two years, yet it had never been my home. There had not been anything of value there for me. It was a gathering place for losers, a spiritual black hole. It was a house of death. Victor Ramos had left there in a vinyl bag; Dean Collins much the same. They were both gone forever, buried in the ground, and I...

I was an ice cube in the sun.

Don't misunderstand, I'm not trying to sell the idea that I had come to some state of grim acceptance of my situation. On the contrary, I was frightened, terrified at the thought of being chipped away a fragment at a time by the elements, malnutrition, and illness. Even my dreams teemed with images of me coughing up the last shreds of my life on the floor of some abandoned building or beaten bloody in an alley by teenagers (punks!) who'd found nothing more in me than a temporary source of entertainment, a brittle bag of bones to provide them with a brief respite from the boredom of waiting for the release of the next new video game.

The dreams got worse when I became homeless because in

the streets I was that much closer to realizing them and because I didn't have to be asleep to dream them. Specters of my ignoble and violent demise dogged my waking hours as vividly as they did when I managed to nod off in the warmth of some apartment building's vestibule, or during the few winks I could steal on a bench at the train depot before an annoyed patrolman hurried me along. I spent a few nights at the rescue mission on Carroll Street, but securing a bed for the night usually meant waiting in a long line of hostile transients. The waiting began as early as three in the afternoon even though admissions didn't start until five and once inside, you were in for the night. The upside was that they provided dinner and breakfast. I didn't realize how hungry I could get until I started living on the street. I didn't get high as much, either. I didn't stop, but the search for a comfortable place to rest imposed a large demand on one's time. I guess that may be considered an upside to homelessness, although it didn't feel like it at the time.

On a cool Sunday afternoon about the middle of the month, I was waiting outside the Deliverance Center at the base of the Southard Street Bridge. Formerly a warehouse, the single-story structure now hosted a variety of energetic worship services, which included lots of crying, screaming, and fainting. I'd been there once before (they serve a delicious southern-style dinner: fried or baked chicken and ham with all the sides, plus dessert—the hook was you had to sit through the service first), and a passionate, touchy-feely Haitian preacher had rubbed my forehead with oil while declaring me cleansed of all unrighteousness.

Yeah, right.

He then pressed the heel of his hand against my forehead and shoved with such force I stumbled backward, trying to maintain balance on my hurting feet in a dance that must have appeared absurdly comical before landing on my backside. The righteous in attendance, however, seemed blown away by the "spirituality" of the spectacle, shouting praises heavenward for another soul saved. I heard somewhere that the preacher's ministrations were what was known as "slaying in the spirit." I had another term for it: assault. I swore I'd never go back there no matter how mouthwatering a spread they offered.

But I was here now for the mouthwatering spread they offered. I was starving. I couldn't remember the last time I'd had a full meal. I was tired and my feet were in agony, hurting more now than ever. Two blocks south of the Deliverance Center was the mission. My mother's house lay two blocks north. Both seemed light years away—especially Momma's.

The shoes I wore were at least a full size too large and I'd cushioned my feet with three pairs of socks, but nothing I tried provided the slightest relief from the constant pain. My every footfall seemed to light upon a bed of nails. It would take an hour to trudge the two measly blocks to the mission only to have to compete with a belligerent crowd for every service from bread to bed, and Momma's, as the last eight weeks had proven, was no longer an option. I had nowhere else to go—and I wasn't in shape to go there if I had.

I sat down on one of the four wrought-iron benches flanking the front entrance to the center. A skinny bearded white guy named Jake sat beside me. I knew Jake, a harmless drunk who eyed me warily as I settled into his space. That's what it comes to for guys like Jake and me. We measure everyone in our immediate proximity for their potential to harm us.

There was a sizable crowd—at least a hundred people—milling about the front of the building waiting for the service to begin. The majority of them were not homeless, although everyone was no doubt hungry. All four benches were occupied; I had only found a seat because the guy there before me wanted to smoke and smoking was prohibited in the paved area directly in front of the center. At least four dozen men and women hovered about the graveled drive encircling the building, puffing away. I hadn't had a cigarette in several days—at least not a whole one. I would sometimes cruise the local hospitals fishing discarded cigs out of smoking area butt cans, but lately I had not been up to the walk. Helene Fuld, the closest, was eight blocks away. It might as well have been on Mars.

I stretched out my legs, pointing my toes upward and thus taking all weight off my hurting soles and for the umpteenth time that day I considered my situation, considered my life. I *was* looking forward to dinner. My belly groaned in anticipation of a meal that didn't consist of shoplifted snack cakes and soda. Dinner here would be the high point of my day, of my week.

And then what? Where will I go from the Deliverance Center? Where will I sleep that night?

God—what's going to happen to me?

I let the questions repeat themselves in my head with no expectation of finding the answers. Maybe I didn't want answers; maybe I already knew them. I lay my head back, letting it perch on the bench's metal backrest. The sunlight felt good on my face and the April sky was pretty. The sunlight always felt good. The sky was always pretty.

I closed my eyes and felt myself melting, an ice cube in the sun. I wouldn't reopen them even when I felt more than heard the commotion commencing around me: the greeters had started conducting the crowd inside. Their welcomes sounded rehearsed but not insincere. Some of the guests responded with peals of grateful laughter. The service would begin in minutes and shortly thereafter, dinner.

The red veil inside my closed eyelids faded to black: someone was standing between me and my sun bath. I opened my eyes to see a tall, big-shouldered man of about sixty smiling down at me.

"Good afternoon, brother, I'm Pastor Kyle." His smile was warm, his tone full of welcome. He extended a freckled hand toward me in greeting. I reached up to shake with him. His grip conveyed a quiet, humble strength.

"I'm Mitch—" I began, but then for some reason it felt wrong to abbreviate my name. "I'm Mitchell."

The blue eyes of the man who'd introduced himself as Pastor Kyle went brilliant with delight. "My *last* name is Mitchell! A fine coincidence, eh?"

No, not really, I thought, but the big guy seemed so pleased with the idea, I nodded, agreeing it was. Our hands were still clasped in greeting and as he spoke, Pastor Kyle Mitchell reached down with his free hand and took me by my elbow, gently helping me to my feet. "Did you know that *Mitchell* in Hebrew means, 'one who is like God'?"

"No," I admitted, "I didn't."

"Oh, yes," Pastor Kyle Mitchell laughed heartily. "It's a good name—a God name and more than a name but a calling to service and to life."

I nodded—it was the only response I could produce. I didn't know what this man was getting at—probably the same nonsense everybody else who'd gone spiritual on me was getting at: Stephanie, some other woman at Momma's church, that Chaplain Tommy from several million years ago.

What is it with all of you, anyway? Can't any of you even see *me? Do I look like somebody fit to serve God? Do I look like someone He'd even want in His service? Serve God? I can't even* walk!

Unmindful of my thoughts and apparently heedless of my suffering personal hygiene, Pastor Kyle put his arm across my shoulders and escorted me inside the building. "Come, Mitchell, my brother in Christ, and share two meals with me."

CHAPTER TWENTY-FOUR

The sanctuary inside the Deliverance Center was a converted storage facility with freshly painted mint-green walls and white trim. More than a hundred meticulously arranged metal folding chairs comprised the pews, each with a Bible on its seat. At the front of the room an electric organ rested beside a complete drum set thoughtfully assembled behind a transparent fiberglass noise shield on a stage only about a foot above floor level. The pulpit was also made of clear fiberglass with the words *Deliverance Ministries* stenciled in white on its front.

Pastor Kyle, his arm still around me, led me to the front pew. There was little competition for this section; most of the evening's congregants were making for the seats in the rear of the room. No doubt some wanted to be as far from the pulpit as possible before it exploded in righteous indignation and moralistic finger-pointing, while others were probably hoping to find a spot where they could nod off unseen by ministerial staff until the sermon was over and it was time to eat. I would have happily joined either group.

Pastor Kyle sat me beside a heavily freckled woman with a mane of fiery red hair. "Mitchell, this is my wife, Danae."

Hesitantly I extended my hand, hoping slow, brief movements would make me less conspicuous to the senses. "Hi."

Danae Mitchell grasped my hand and held it warmly, even placing her other hand on my shoulder to emphasize her sincerity. "Welcome, Mitchell."

Her smile was even wider than her husband's. Her hazel eyes smiled too, tiny wrinkles appearing at their corners. I smiled back, relaxing a little in spite of myself.

As the assembly began to settle down, three young people approached the stage, walking from the rear of the sanctuary up the center aisle. One of them (who anyone could see was the son of Kyle and Danae Mitchell) was carrying an acoustic guitar. The other two, a young man in his twenties and a girl—probably also related to the Mitchells—assumed places at the drums and keyboards respectively.

From a recessed track in the ceiling above and behind the pulpit, a screen descended as the boy with the guitar positioned himself at a mic stand between his fellow musicians.

"Good afternoon, everybody!" he greeted cheerily, and the assembly responded in kind, many of them applauding as well. The boy smiled—Danae's smile—and after striking a few opening chords on his guitar commanded: "Let's rise to our feet and praise the Lord!"

More applause as the congregation stood. I left my seat with deliberate quickness and feigned ease so as not to betray the pain in my feet. I didn't want the pastor's wife to know. I didn't like the idea of appearing afflicted and weak in front of this woman.

From a projector somewhere in the rear of the room song lyrics appeared on the screen and the congregation began to sing:

Open the eyes of my heart, Lord
Open the eyes of my heart
I want to see you, I want to see you

Many of those present apparently knew the song; others were clearly faking it. I'd never heard it before. It seemed to me one of those contemporary white Christian songs sung in one of those contemporary white Christian churches I'd never have occasion to attend. In any case, I'd never heard it at my church—former church.

I'd never really considered the differences in worship styles between blacks and whites, except that black services were too long and whites too dull; but to each their own. Still, I couldn't help feeling a little disappointed they hadn't selected a song I knew. I've been told I can carry a tune and would not have minded a chance to impress Danae Mitchell. For the moment I faked it as did many others, lip-synching as I adjusted to the mild culture shock of contemporary praise and worship.

To see You high and lifted up
Shining in the light of Your glory
Pour out Your power and love
As we sing holy, holy, holy

But the melody was simple enough and the lyrics were right in front of me. When we halfway through the song for the second time, I was singing as though I'd known it all my life.

Holy, holy, holy,
Holy, holy, holy,
Holy, holy, holy,
I want to see you.

The song ended and we all applauded; some even cheered. I clapped too, feeling pretty good and forgetting for the moment my pain and hunger.

Forgetting—for the moment—everything.

The three-person band launched into another number as the lyrics on the screen changed. A satisfied smile played across my face. This one I knew:

Amazing grace, how sweet the sound,
That saved a wretch like me,
I once was lost, but now I'm found,
Was blind, but now I see

As a member of the male chorus at Momma's church, I'd sung lead on that song. It seemed so long ago now, a different man's life in a different world. I thought about how good I felt at the lead mic, the compliments I received from church members after, and how proud Mom had been. The memory began a stirring inside me that I was in no mood to entertain. I repressed it and poured myself into my singing.

My chains are gone, I've been set free
My God, my Savior has ransomed me
And like a flood His mercy reigns
Unending love, amazing grace

More cheers and applause as the song concluded, none more heartfelt than my own. I looked over at Danae Mitchell, thinking to tell her how well the band played while hoping to elicit a compliment about my singing. She was smiling but not like before—not happily. Now there was only a gentle curl of her mouth accompanied by a deep sympathetic sadness in her eyes. I guess I hadn't been successful in concealing my pain after all.

With a soft electronic hum the screen returned to its resting place in the ceiling. By this time Pastor Kyle Mitchell had addressed the pulpit, a large burgundy-colored Bible in his hands. The congregation fell silent and for the first time I became aware of food aromas from the adjoining kitchen/dining area. I was so hungry my stomach hurt. I hoped Danae Mitchell couldn't hear its protests, although I was fairly certain she could. This was one of those times I could scarcely believe what a complete and total mess I was.

As if commiserating with my—and I suspect many others'—discomfort, Kyle Mitchell patted his stomach and grinned. "My tank just asked if I were done preaching yet."

Appreciative laughter and clapping among the congregation. I laughed too. Pastor Kyle had a way with people. He could inspire comfort and ease in a tense or anxious crowd—probably not a useless talent for someone in the business of telling people things they usually didn't want to hear. He placed his big Bible atop the inclined surface of the podium as he spoke.

"I've always been more a fan of long lunches than long sermons."

More laughter.

"So what do you say we share a brief meal from here"—he patted the Bible and then aimed his thumb at the dining room—"and then a bigger one in there?"

The congregation cheered its approval and then quieted as Pastor Kyle opened the Bible and began thumbing through the pages. "Please turn with me to the Gospel of Saint Mark, chapter five, beginning at verse one."

I fished my dollar-store reading glasses from my jacket pocket. The cheap wire frames were bent and the lenses scuffed, but they were better than nothing. I put them on and examined the Bible I'd found on my seat and had been holding all the while for the first time: a soft cover New International Version with (thankfully) large print. I opened it and turned to the table of contents. I didn't know offhand the location of the passage Pastor Kyle mentioned, but it had a familiar ring, as if it had attached itself to my awareness at some former time and not let go.

Kyle Mitchell waited, listening as the rustling of pages gradually ceased. I suspect I was among the last to find the scripture address. Then I stared, total recall kicking in as I read the heading of chapter five:

The Healing of a Demon-Possessed Man

It was the passage from that tract Chaplain Tommy gave me that night at the hospital. I'd read only part of it but had never been able to bring myself to toss it. I left it on the makeshift night table (an upended milk crate draped with a towel and topped with an album cover from War's *Deliver the Word*) beside my scavenged bed in my former basement hovel. I'd told myself that Redman needed it more than I, that he was a more deceitful, more despicable, more disreputable person for putting me out after all I did for him, the drugs I gave to him and shared with him, and the money I paid to live in his basement. *His basement.*

Pastor Kyle Mitchell looked out over his seated guests as he donned a pair of slim, gold-framed glasses, and then in a voice I barely recognized as that of the jovial preacher who had greeted me, read:

"1. They went across the lake to the region of the Gerasenes. 2. When Jesus got out of the boat, a man with an evil spirit cam to meet him. 3. This man lived in the tombs, and no one could bind him anymore, not even with a chain. 4. For he had often been chained hand and foot, but he tore the chains apart and broke the irons at his feet. No one was strong enough to subdue him. 5. Night and day among the tombs and in the hills he would cry out and cut himself with stones.

"6. When he saw Jesus from a distance, he ran and fell on his knees in front of him. 7. He shouted at the top of his voice, 'What do you want with me, Jesus, Son of the Most High God? Swear to God you won't torture me!' 8. For Jesus had said to him, 'Come out of this man, evil spirit!'"

The pastor stopped reading and looked up from the big red book to survey the room over the top of his glasses. After a moment he removed the glasses from the bridge of his sharp, prominent nose, left the pulpit and dismounted the stage to come to within arm's length of the front row. His gaze seemed to fall upon every face in the room (taking care, I thought, not to linger too long on mine) as he began his sermon. "A strange thing happened last night as I sat down to prepare this message: I found myself considering the man in this passage in a way I never did before. Maybe it was the lateness of the hour plus the fatigue I felt after having spent a long day in ministry. Whatever the cause, this man—this demon-possessed man—took on a depth and dimension in my mind that he never had in all the years I've read and preached from this particular story." He paused, focusing intently on his audience and then continued. "Suddenly I'm preoccupied with questions about this man. Questions that compelled me to see him in three dimensions, not just as a character in a story, but a flesh and blood human being. A man not unlike myself, a man maybe not so different from some of you." Now the pastor began to pace along the center aisle, hands behind him, one resting in the other. "But I won't presume to speak for any of you. Instead, I'll just share with you some of the questions that came to me and let you decide for yourself—is that fine with you?"

I don't know if the pastor was really expecting an answer; he got it nonetheless in the form of nodding heads and a few affirming comments among his congregation for the evening. Kyle Mitchell nodded, acknowledging the response, and went on.

"The first thing I wondered was: What kind of person was this man before this terrible thing—this possession happened to him?" Again the pastor paused, letting the question settle in the minds of the audience. "Was he a bad person, an evil man given to evil thoughts and evil deeds and so through his wickedness invited this demonic invasion of his person? Or was he a good man—a *godly* man, even; one who loved and provided for his family and who worshipped and prayed and walked with God? A man who through no fault of his own merely fell victim to the evil that overtook him? I ask that because having an evil thing happen to you doesn't automatically prove you're an evil person. Sometimes bad things happen to good people, am I right?"

More nodding heads and agreeing comments answered the pastor who had now begun to pace down the center aisle. "Unfortunately, this text does not provide the necessary background information for us to reach a decision about the character of this man prior to the events in the story. There's no way we can know for certain what kind of man he was. We can only speculate and guess—but so what? I'll bet more than a few of you know how it feels to be talked about by people who don't know a thing about you, yes?"

Someone a few rows behind me yelled, "You got *that* right!" sparking a chorus of chatter and chuckles among the crowd. Pastor Kyle nodded knowingly and continued.

"I then wondered about the possession itself: How did this happen to him—was it a gradual occurrence? Did these demons strip away this man's sanity in layers: bits of memory one day, basic cognitive skills the next, and then finally his ability to reason?

"Or did they seize him suddenly and quickly? Did he go to bed in perfect right mind one night only to wake that next morning screaming obscenities and foaming at the mouth?" He stopped raised his hands palms-up in an exaggerated shrug. "Again, my friends, there's not enough information here to answer the question. We can wonder; we can't really know." He resumed his idle trek back up the aisle toward the pulpit, turning to walk past the row where his wife and I sat. As he passed, I studied Pastor Kyle Mitchell carefully. He was a lean man with a bit of a paunch beneath a plain white shirt and tan corduroy blazer with jeans and loafers to complete the comfy/casual ensemble. His face was clean shaven and sported a dimpled chin. Except for his close-cropped silver-gray hair, he didn't appear a man in his sixties. He struck me as man who'd seen much—good and bad—and had not only been strengthened by both, but had kept his family close to share it with. I envied him.

Kyle Mitchell resumed his speech, folding his arms across his chest. "Lastly, I wondered if he knew what was happening to him. Was there somewhere in him a place of awareness where he was able to appreciate the gravity of his situation even if he was unable to do anything to do anything about it? In other words, did he know he was losing his mind even while he was losing it?"

That evidently caught some guests off guard as their varied responses indicated. I was curiously affected by the pastor's reference to the man's insanity as well. It started a strange/familiar stirring in my stomach that was decidedly not hunger-related.

The pastor unfolded his arms and stood as if tensed to receive whatever negative returns his remark invoked. "And that question, my friends—as troubling as it seems for some of you—is the only of the three we can answer based on the information provided in the passage.

"Now I know the idea of someone losing his mind carries a certain shock value, and I don't mean to shock or offend anyone. But let's look at the man in this story with honest eyes, shall we? The Bible describes him as demon-possessed, living in the tombs, crying in the night, and cutting himself with stones. Is there anyone here who doesn't agree that sounds just a little crazy?"

Mumbled responses of concurrence, a nervous laugh here and there, but no one disagreed. Pastor Kyle stood with the pulpit at his back and the congregation before him. His hands went to rest in his pants pockets, making his wide shoulders appear once more as though shrugging.

"I think he knew—knew in his heart and in his spirit—that something evil was happening to him. I believe he could feel his sanity slipping, feel his thoughts, his behavior; feel his *body* falling under the control of forces he couldn't resist or even understand.

"Does that sound strange, a little far-fetched to some of you? I can understand how it might. But before you decide you can't identify with our friend in the tombs, I want to challenge you to put yourselves in his shoes for a moment. I challenge you to imagine that you are a victim of demonic possession, that for whatever reason evil spirits have entered your bodies and taken over, controlling your thoughts, your actions, your life."

At that the room became silent—deathly still, except for the moving about in my stomach, which had progressed from a subtle stirring to an irritated squirming. Alarmed, I crossed my arms over my abdomen, hoping to quell or at least conceal the activity.

"It's likely you would not immediately guess the nature of the strange thoughts and feelings you're having," the pastor explained. "You would probably not automatically associate feeling strangely with the presence of demonic forces inside you. I mean, it's not as though they circulated a flyer announcing they were moving into the neighborhood. After all, these are evil spirits we're talking about—not a new pizza parlor."

More than a few people found that funny. The preacher smiled, waiting for the sporadic laughter to subside before going on. "But you know that *something* is wrong. You're having feelings you don't understand and thoughts you don't like. You're starting to do things you can't believe you're doing. Your very personality seems to be changing—everything about you is changing.

"The people who know you best and love you most look at you with worry and fear in their eyes. They comment on your behavior and ask if you're all right. They're afraid *for* you and afraid *of* you.

"And you're afraid as well. You've become a stranger to yourself and you don't know why. All you know for sure is that something is wrong—very wrong—with you." He stopped, brilliant blue eyes gazing about the room to meet with the expectant stares of his audience. "Maybe none of you knows how that feels ... maybe some of you know someone who does."

I heard a whimper—more than one—rise in the still of the sanctuary. It seemed Pastor Kyle Mitchell had found a commiserate heart or two in the room. I think one of them might have been mine.

"Try to imagine how frightened, how terrified this man must have felt. Having his reason, his personality, his very identity stripped away and unable to make sense of it. How many times did this poor man look in the mirror and ask, 'What's happening to me?' and when he did, was he even able to recognize his own reflection?" Here the pastor paused and looked up, as though requiring permission from on high to proceed. Then he returned his attention to the assembly, his consent apparently granted.

"Let me ask you: Have you ever felt lost and afraid? Have you ever felt so alone and frightened you thought you were on the verge of a breakdown?"

A collective response of affirmatives circulated the room, mumbles of confirmation and bobbing heads with hands raised high in the air. A female voice from somewhere to my right called "Amen!" in a voice that was choked, full of emotion.

"And do you know what a breakdown is?" Pastor Kyle asked and went on before anyone could reply. "A breakdown is a mind caving in to insurmountable pressure or stress; an anguished and desperate plea for help, for peace. For this man in the tombs it was crying and cutting himself with stones." He waited, raising a hand to stifle the groans of dismay coming from several places in the pews. "Yes, I know how hard that is to comprehend: dwelling in dead places, cutting himself with stones. I have trouble understanding it too. I hear about young people—mostly teenage girls—cutting themselves with knives and razors, and I have trouble understanding that as well. We can't always know what's going on in the minds of people who do things to harm themselves. Like those who deliberately give themselves over to abusive relationships, or those who give in to the impulse to take their own lives, or those who become slaves in addiction to drugs and alcohol."

Slaves, I thought. I was ashamed and lowered my head before anyone could see. *Slaves.*

"But my heart tells me that the spirit of a person will react one way or another when oppressed by other spirits," Pastor Kyle declared. "Spirits with no less purpose than to kill the body they've invaded and kill the life they've taken over. When I consider the countless styles of self-abuse and self-destruction being practiced these days, cutting oneself with stones seems downright tame by comparison, doesn't it?"

At that the congregation applauded. I thought to join them but could only nod as the demon-possessed man in the pastor's sermon began to assume greater depth and dimension in my thinking—just as he had in the pastor's.

My relationship with the church had been superficial at best. I'd never given enough of myself in study or worship to appreciate the characters in Bible stories as real people. It wasn't unbelief, not precisely, but a sense of disconnection, an inability to relate to people and events more than two thousand years in the past. I believed in them. I just didn't *know* them.

But this man—this demon-possessed man Kyle Mitchell so clearly illustrated—he was becoming more than just some long-dead character in an ancient tale. He seemed—no, *felt*—he felt closer.

"When something that strange to you—when something that *unlike* you—is going on inside you," Pastor Kyle preached again, "you know it. You can't help but know it. And I can't help wondering if this man—this spirit-besieged man had tried to convey his confusion and fear to others. I wonder if—when he could still form the words—he tried to explain to someone what he was feeling, what he was going through. I wonder if—before he resorted to the crying and cutting and tomb-dwelling—he had tried to reach out to someone—a friend, neighbor, or relative—begged someone to see his private suffering and step forward to save him."

Someone behind me was crying; unashamed, unbound wails of deep, soul-stirring anguish filling the air around me. I didn't need to look to know it was the mournful wail of a mother for her child. I thought of my own mother and my heart sank. Was she thinking of me? Worrying about me?

Was she mournfully wailing for me?

I know I've already said it. It bears—demands—repeating: addiction is a selfish lifestyle. The addict—the junkie—has just one concern: to feed his demons, to worship his gods. His is a single-minded, by-any-means-necessary ambition that far outweighs every other consideration. A child in need, a mother in tears, a family in turmoil, a home in ruins—none even come close in priority.

Sometimes in that still and quiet space of time between darkest and dawn, he may consider those he has disappointed or betrayed and for that time entertain moral burdens such as guilt and regret, but that time, though interminable, does pass, leaving the junkie alone with his gods. His demanding, greedy gods.

"And if this frightened, stricken man did indeed reach out in his desperation and fear for the help he needed," Pastor Kyle preached on, "what was the response of those he reached out to? Was it one born of love, understanding, and compassion? Or did they seek to 'help' him by chaining him hand and foot like a sick animal, a mad dog ..." He was still speaking even as the congregation exploded in cheers and applause. I was applauding too, the significance of the pastor's words resounding in my head and filling my heart. At that moment I think I identified more with that man—that demon-possessed man—than with any person I'd ever known.

Kyle Mitchell raised his hands, motioning the crowd to quiet down. Gradually silence reigned again. "In the scripture verses we see words like 'restrain' and 'subdued' with respect to the people's treatment of that stricken man. I find that such words reflect an attitude prevalent in today's society. We continue to treat the sick and suffering among us by warehousing them in prisons or turning them into docile and mindless zombies with 'behavior modifying' drugs ..."

Or putting them in rehabs, I thought dully.

"... or committing them to institutions." At this point Pastor Kyle appeared angry: pacing back and forth in the area between the stage and the front pew and seemingly speaking more to himself than his listeners. For a moment it seemed as though he'd forgotten we were there. "Billions are spent building more and more places to house the afflicted and the result is little to no success and why?" He stopped now—as if suddenly remembering he was addressing a room full of people. "Because our concern is with 'restraining' and 'controlling' the afflicted, when it's supposed to be with *healing* them—lifting them up to God for His healing!"

Now the crowd was on its feet, all but drowning out the preacher with applause. Pastor stood before them and waited, hands in his pockets again. The anger had drained out of his features. Now he looked sad. "And so what we have is a sustained and growing condition of sickness in our communities, our neighborhoods, and our homes. The suffering of one becomes the suffering of many—the suffering of all. We make vain and desperate attempts to 'restrain' and 'subdue' the disorder without seeking God's counsel and when we do that, my friends, we only perpetuate the disorder. We all get sick—we all *stay* sick."

"That's right!" one man shouted, and at the same time I heard myself sigh, "That's right."

Pastor Kyle made a final pass down the center aisle. All eyes in the house were on him—all except mine. I'd lowered my gaze to the floor, seeing in my mind that demon-possessed man lying on a dirty mattress in a dank basement sticking a needle in his arm.

"And so he dwells in the tombs." The pastor had lowered his voice, compelling any chatter—not that there was any, as you could hear the proverbial pin drop—to cease that he could be heard. "Making his home among the dead because there's no place for him among the living. He spends his days hurting himself and his nights crying out in anguish. His life is in ruins, his soul is in torment, and so he cries. Does anyone here know what it's like to hurt like that? To cry like that?

One woman cried out—a sound I can only describe as anguished. Another screamed "Yes!" over and over. Even before Pastor Kyle mentioned living among the dead my thoughts were in that house where I had "dwelled" for two years. I thought about the people—men and women and even children—who came and went, conducting their depraved and wretched business, willing to do anything, risk anything for a moment of ... what?

I thought about Victor Ramos and Dean Collins—both dead. I thought about me—lying on a soiled mattress in the basement of that place—nearly dead from an overdose. I shuddered, the enormity of it all draping over me like a blanket—a grave blanket.

That place—that basement—that house was a tomb, a place of the dead. And now I didn't even have that. I had been evicted from a tomb. I had nothing.

I wanted to shout, to cry out my anguish like the man in the story. I rose from my chair and stood on my unsteady, ruined feet, clutching that Bible to my chest. I was trembling; my eyes were stinging. I squeezed them shut against the flood welling inside me and prayed I wouldn't collapse.

"The crying of a soul in torment," Pastor Kyle reiterated. "A soul at the end of its endurance, crying out for healing, peace, and rest. A soul crying out for Jesus."

"Jesus!" one woman cried, then another, and then a man—until the name was passing and echoing endlessly throughout the room. The crowd seemed unwilling to let it fade to silence.

"Jesus," I whispered and instantly understood everyone's obsession with the name. Just speaking it seemed to invoke an unexplainable feeling of ease, a peace that transcended my comprehension.

No—it was more than that. The name seemed to move the very atmosphere, filling everything with its power. It ignited, burned, a fierce, all-consuming flame in my spirit and in my flesh, shutting up in my bones.

Yes and even more than that. The name—that Name—called to me, invited me to rest in it. It spoke to me a promise, an assurance I couldn't begin to fathom. It touched off a yearning, a hunger deep inside me.

"Jesus," I said again, and the Name only became stronger for the repetition, lingering sweetly and powerfully on my lips.

And something was happening to me—happening *in* me.

Until then my relationship with Jesus had been as superficial and shallow as my relationship with the church. It wasn't unbelief, not exactly, but a sense of distance, a failure to bridge the span of the centuries to share kinship with Him in the now. To my mind Jesus had been the hero of a former age, the Lord of a bygone era. He was, to great extent, the folklore of my ancestors.

No—"folklore" isn't the right word; it inaccurately implies unbelief and it wasn't that I didn't believe in Jesus. I just didn't know Him.

Suddenly now—at the end of my endurance—at the very bottom of my existence I felt connected to Him, united with Him through the insanity of a man who lived and died two millennia ago.

And I'm back then, back where he was, dwelling in the tombs, crying out in anguish, and cutting myself with stones.

For a few minutes the commotion, the outbursts, the shrieks, the moans, and crying continued without interruption from Pastor Kyle. The name Jesus is called over and over, echoing seemingly forever inside that place. I muttered something—for the life of me I don't know what—I couldn't hear myself over the restless rumblings in my belly.

They were in pain. The gods of addiction were in pain. I could sense their suffering, taste their agony. With my eyes closed I could almost see them—trying to squirm away from the Name, trying to escape into my nether region, worm through my depths. Trying to bury themselves in my bowels like swine in a muddy sty.

Trying to hide from the light.

In agony, yes, and frightened. The gods were terrified.

It…tickled.

I bowed my head and leaned toward the image for a closer look, trying to discern detail among their writhing shadowy forms. I wanted to see the expressions of horror on their wicked faces, look into their terrified evil eyes, and watch them suffer.

I wanted to watch the gods of addiction die.

"When I started this sermon I asked what sort of person this man in the tombs was." The pastor's voice—clear and close by—drew me away from my vengeful vigil. I kept my eyes closed, envisioning him next to me, perhaps talking to me. "But I say now that it doesn't matter what kind of person he was before. It doesn't matter what sin he'd committed or what crime he was guilty of. If it mattered, the writer of this passage would have mentioned it.

"But not a word about the man's past appears in the story, because Jesus didn't care who he'd been or where he came from. He didn't ask what high school the man attended, if he had a criminal record or what his credit score was. Jesus didn't concern Himself with whether the man had been abandoned by his father, abused by his mother, or if he beat his dog.

"Jesus didn't need to read his psychiatric profile in order to prescribe his treatment plan." Each comment brought more enthusiastic applause than the one it followed. Shouts of "Halleluiah!" and "Praise Jesus!" rose toward heaven in endless repetition.

"Jesus," I moaned around a lump of emotion in my throat. Then I became aware that I was not alone. I opened my eyes. Pastor Kyle Mitchell was standing in front of me. I looked into the preacher's eyes and suddenly no longer felt desolate or afraid. I held the pastor's gaze with my own, a strong feeling of anticipation kindling inside me for what he would say next—and where it would take me.

"Ah, the power in that name, my friends, the wonder-working power in that name. Power to heal any affliction and remove any infirmity. In that name—the mighty name of Jesus—is the power to ease all suffering and command any spirit. A power not demonstrated through chains and restraints, by the shedding of His own precious blood and the laying down of His life. Because of Him we don't have to be trapped in dysfunction and disorder; we don't have to be defeated by sickness and disease. By His stripes sin and death have lost their power to claim us, and all who come to Him find life."

It was obvious to all now that this man, this preacher, was speaking to me, directly and unmistakably to me. But I felt no shame, only a deep, inner need to believe his words were indeed for me.

"I tell you now, healing is as close as your desire to believe in Him; wholeness as near as your decision to trust Him. I invite you to come forth. Bring your affliction, your suffering, to Jesus. He's waiting for you, my friend. Waiting to make you whole, waiting to make you free." He held out his hand to me and smiled, a soft, reassuring curl of the corners of his mouth. The preacher fairly glowed with the power of the words he'd spoken, the sheer joy of the undeniable and eternal Truth he knew. I nodded, mumbled some unintelligible, hopeful thing, thinking how fine it must be to feel that certain, that sure. I thought, *What I wouldn't do to know what he knows and feel what he feels.*

Slowly I stepped forward, reaching my bony hand out to take his.

The congregation roared in celebration.

And the gods of addiction shrieked in agony.

CHAPTER TWENTY-FIVE

The service ended with the congregation singing "Lord, I Lift Your Name on High," a song with which I was reasonably familiar, but I was too overcome to join in singing. I sat while everyone else stood, feeling glad and grateful and tired and anxious and confused and...scared too, I think, but it seemed an incidental fear, without strength or teeth; a fear that didn't scare me.

I fixed my gaze on the Bible in my hands. Before delivering the benediction, Pastor Kyle had told us we were welcome to keep them. He then began to conduct the congregation-turned-dinner-guests next door for the evening meal. The keyboard player (who, I later learned, was the pastor's daughter) along with her husband (the drummer) went with him, their ministry continuing on the serving line alongside a dozen additional volunteers. Watching them leave, I suddenly realized that Danae was still sitting beside me, her arm around my shoulders. I looked toward her, half-stunned to find her there.

"Let's get you something to eat," she said softly.

I was still ravenously hungry but not ready to go just yet. I told the kind preacher's woman that I'd be along; I just wanted to sit for a while. Thankfully she seemed to understand. She rose, granting my request for privacy.

"I'm happy for you, Mitchell," the good woman said and then went to join her family in the dining room.

I sat in the silence of the sanctuary with the roar of my thoughts as every sermon, every message, and every testimony I'd ever heard came alive in my mind. Long-forgotten and half-heard Bible passages attesting to the goodness, grace, and mercy of God revisited my memory completely and accurately, not so much as a comma out of place. Hymns I'd heard only once sung themselves in their entirety, and even the simplest, most elementary Sunday school rhymes rang in my spirit with fresh new meaning. As I said before, I'm no stranger to the church, still I couldn't believe I had retained so much, that it had all been inside me, waiting to reacquaint me with Him and reassert His truth to me.

I ran my fingers along the raised NIV on the cover of the Bible—*my* Bible

Could it be that simple? I marveled. Could thirty years of addiction, three decades of single-minded devotion to the worship of greedy, heartless gods be wiped away and a wasted life restored simply because I came to believe?

The answer came as a refreshing whisper of a breeze through my mind.

I'm not a junkie.

Not anymore.

Not ever again.

I sat my Bible on my lap and looked at my hands, turning them over and back as if searching for some sign of change. They looked the same: ashen and bony with ragged nails and nicotine-stained fingertips. The rest of me was the same as well: underweight and weather-beaten, in dire need of a shower, fresh clothing, and a hot meal—a few hot meals.

But I *was* different—changed because somehow I'd been connected, related to some crying, self-mutilating lunatic in a graveyard centuries in the past, the veil of my own insanity and suffering pierced by his so that I could see.

So that I could see Him—not as some distant semimythical figure out of ancient history— but as Lord of right here and right now.

And I knew. I knew that Jesus was with me. I knew it with far greater certainty than I'd ever had about anything. And knowing— just knowing—brought with it an indescribable feeling of peace I wouldn't have believed possible for a man in my predicament: a forty-seven-year-old black man with a history—a life—of drug abuse and criminal activity.

I'd seen things I knew I'd never reveal, done things I'd never confess to any human being. I knew things I'd gladly gouge out of my brain if I could. I had no province, no prospects, and no plan. I didn't know where my next meal was coming from or where I would lay my head that night.

But I knew I wasn't a junkie—not anymore.

And so I wasn't afraid—not anymore.

Momma told me that God knows the desires of the heart, and that He would provide. I believed it now—against everything I knew to be reasonable, I believed. I didn't know what He had in mind for me, had no idea where He would take me from there. But I knew—I knew—I would never again give myself away to drugs and alcohol.

Hello, my name is Mitchell and I'm not an addict

I smiled with the thought. And I knew. I knew that God would provide.

"I hope you're hungry."

I was still smiling when I turned toward the sound of Pastor Kyle Mitchell's voice. He had removed the blazer and was wearing an apron, the words "God loves the cook" silk-screened across the front. His shirt sleeves were rolled up, exposing fine silver hairs on his forearms. He didn't look like any preacher I ever knew. When I took his hand during the service, he didn't seize on the moment to display me before the congregation like a puppy he'd paper-trained. He merely leaned toward me, touching his cheek to mine as he whispered in my ear. Then he let me resume my seat. I was grateful for that.

"I said I hope you're hungry," the preacher repeated grinning. "Danae is holding a plate for you. God bless that woman—she piles it on like there's no tomorrow."

I took my new Bible in both hands and stood. I'd forgotten how hungry I was, forgotten that the food had been my sole purpose for coming to the center. Now the acids in my stomach conspired to remind me how long it had been since I had a meal.

"I'm ready," I said and walked to the dining room with the pastor, who stayed close to me despite my ailing personal hygiene.

CHAPTER TWENTY-SIX

Danae Mitchell was indeed a woman who prepared meals without regard for plate capacity or portion control. The one she set before me was a culinary monument: baked chicken, honey baked ham, *and* roast beef plus green beans, corn on the cob, and mashed potatoes. Raw baby carrots, celery sticks, and a spattering of black olives had been added for nutritional balance, and a huge dinner roll completed the meal; a veritable mountain of food more to be climbed than consumed, and as hungry as I was, I knew I'd never be able to take it all in. Too many missed meals had shrunk my stomach to roughly the size of a change purse. Still, out of gratitude, for politeness' sake and *because* I was hungry, I ate as much as I could, chewing thoroughly and making it my business to taste at least some of everything on my plate, including the raw vegetables.

There was no serving line, no queue of hungry guests pushing and shoving for position. The congregation had been instructed to be seated at tables spread with checkered cloths and set with paper napkins and plastic utensils while volunteers (members of Pastor Kyle's church in Bordentown) hopped from table to table carrying trays loaded with food. They were the very heart and soul of ministry: courteous and patient with their ravenous guests and happy to serve. Enticingly positioned on the far side of the room was a long conference table draped with white linen and laden with a variety of cakes, pies, and pastries.

Pastor Kyle said very little as we ate. When he did speak it was to answer a question or respond to a comment on his sermon posed by a passing guest. I hadn't said more than half a dozen words since being introduced by the pastor to his kids and son-in-law. At one point Danae appeared to ask if either her husband or I wanted more. She glanced at my plate and saw the slow progress I'd made with my meal but made no comment. I suppose she understood.

Surprisingly, I was able to eat more than I initially believed I could. If I applied myself, I thought, I could finish at least most of it plus a piece of that decadent-looking coconut cake I saw making rounds of the room—and maybe a piece of pie to go at least.

"How do you feel?" Pastor Kyle Mitchell finally asked, and he may as well have been inquiring as to how many rocks there were on Pluto. It wasn't that I didn't know how I felt; it was that I felt so many things and couldn't narrow it down to one in particular. A host of emotions were competing for dominance inside me. I felt glad and apprehensive, elated and fatigued, changed yet the same. Again I felt scared—but then not really, not very.

"Pretty good," I said and immediately felt stupid with the reply. I couldn't have come up with a more inadequate, insufficient answer if I'd tried. If the pastor was unsatisfied, however, I couldn't tell from his expression.

"Ready?" he asked after another silent moment and the one-word question was as provocative as my two-word response had been dumb. I looked up from my plate, the potential import of the question playing havoc with my newfound peace.

"Sir?"

He was sitting directly across the table from me. He placed his fork beside his plate and rested his arms one atop the other on the table.

"Are you ready to answer God's calling on your life?"

I looked at the pastor, unsure how to respond.

My descent into madness had been such a subtle and gradual process I didn't know it was happening. Even today as I look back on my life I see my fall from innocence to iniquity as an almost blameless occurrence.

I don't remember how old I was when I took my first drink or smoked my first joint. Hanging out with my boys and getting high on weekends seemed to be an activity you just naturally grew into, a rite of passage no more wicked than getting your driver's permit or growing that first hair on your chin. Getting high was fun; it wasn't wrong.

I remember experimenting with hallucinogenics and similar drugs in the '70s and joining a crowd in the marines who I considered worldly and wise. I was seventeen, rather large for my age, and eager to prove to my new peer group that I was not a dumb kid; I belonged with them. They were a rebellious, angry bunch— angry at everyone, most especially whites, for every misfortune and misery of their lives. As their fledgling recruit I aspired to be as rebellious and angry as they, blaming the world for suffering I'd never known and medicating myself as a means for expressing a resentment I didn't truly harbor against a community that had done me no harm.

I do remember the first time I stuck a needle in my arm. It was the logical next step in my devolution, I suppose. I was out of the service by then, discharged several years, and my temperament was well conditioned at that point to embrace the concept of intravenous drug use. I think maybe I even enjoyed it once, although I can't quite recall when—contrary to what you may hear in other testimonies, however, I did not enjoy my first time.

I'm forever amazed at how quickly time passes, how those years sped by. I recall with great dismay my descent into deceit, dishonesty, and depravity, finding myself in places I couldn't imagine existed and doing things I didn't believe I was capable of doing. I remember my betrayals against those who loved and trusted me, my innumerable brushes with the law—and with death.

And it all came so naturally. So innocently.

But I haven't been blameless for many years or sane for far more. Later down the road a preacher would explain to me that iniquity is sin that goes unresolved in a person's life so that it *becomes* his life; little by little displacing all that is good and decent and righteous about him as it justifies itself, robbing him of his joy, his sanity, and finally his life.

I look back on my life and think: that's about the size of it, all right. My life: a life of iniquity, of unresolved sin and insanity. Quite a sizable burden to put down, a long way back from which to come...

A lot for which to ask forgiveness. A lot for which to *be* forgiven; yet in my heart I know that I am forgiven. In my spirit I know that I'm healed.

I know that Jesus has driven the gods of addiction out of me. I can feel His presence; I know He's with me. For the first time in my life I feel He does have a plan for me.

I thought about what Pastor Kyle had whispered to me near the end of the service. I looked into his eyes and nodded.

"I just don't know what He wants me to do," I said, a simple and honest statement of fact conveying neither hesitation nor fear, only the truth. "I don't know where He wants me to start."

Now it was the pastor's turn to nod, his head slowly accepting my dilemma as he thought it over. He was about to speak when

Danae—that delightful woman—came to the table bringing two large slabs of coconut cake. Without a word she set them before us and hurried away to serve others with my heartfelt "Thank you" trailing after her.

Neither the pastor nor I said a word before tasting our dessert—which was as delicious as it looked. We ate in silence for a moment. I hoped he wouldn't believe I was making him the repository of my troubles. He'd already been so gracious; I felt I owed him a great deal more than I could ever pay. Still, I couldn't help feeling anxious—if he had a suggestion…

Pastor Kyle Mitchell put his fork down again. He laced his fingers on the table in front of him, blue eyes blazing brilliantly as he smiled.

"When it comes to the business of God, I've always found that a good place to start—the very best place to start—is home."

CHAPTER TWENTY-SEVEN

An eerie feeling came over me as I said good-bye to Pastor Kyle Mitchell and his family. I was seized by a sudden and unexplainable sense of mourning, a sorrowful conviction that I'd never see any of them again. I know how ridiculously vain this is liable to sound and I can't begin to guess why I felt that way—but it was as though the Mitchells had only existed on earth for that brief span of time I knew them because they had only existed *for* me, that God had dispatched five of His angels with the specific purpose of saving me.

Danae hugged me as though I were an old and cherished friend. She told me again how happy she was for me. There were tears in her kind eyes as she implored me to trust in God; He would see me through. I shared hearty handshakes with son David and son-in-law Freddie Kline, and daughter Patricia Kline hugged me as affectionately as did her mother. Then the family seemed to fade back as daddy Pastor Kyle walked with me to the pavement leading off the center grounds. He gave my shoulder a firm squeeze with his left hand as his right clasped mine in farewell. I wanted to ask him what and how he knew about God's "calling" on my life. Strangely, though, I felt as though posing the question—even though it concerned me—would be intrusive, like the answer was between the pastor and God and none of my business.

Bible in hand, I headed for Bond Street. I didn't look back. That odd feeling had come back to harass me again. I almost believed that if I turned around I'd find not only Pastor Kyle and his family, but the Deliverance Center itself had vanished, with not even the benches and driveway left behind to prove it had ever been. Again, I don't know why I felt that way; I just did, and the last couple of hours had been mystical and miraculous enough for me.

Pastor Kyle had been right. I needed to go home. I don't know what God hand in mind for me, but I was sure it would include making things right with my family.

I missed them. I didn't appreciate the enormity of being apart from them until Momma shut me out. My brothers and sisters had all but given up on me long ago, but Mom was always my way back in, my last line of defense. I never really felt disconnected from the others as long as I had her. I never took the time to consider what it must have taken to push her to the point where she had to reject me. I'd been too caught up in my addiction, too concerned with dwelling in self-pity and paying tribute to my gods to care about the pain I was causing those who loved me.

I had to make that right and ask her—ask them all—to forgive me.

As I made the intersection of Southard Street and Brunswick Avenue it occurred to me that Momma might not be willing to listen, that she wouldn't forgive me. I didn't believe it, but then I didn't believe it when she left me out in the cold that night in February. I'd put her through so much. *What if she really is through with me? What if this attempt to make amends is much too little, far too late?*

With a heavy heart I decided it didn't matter. I couldn't make any of them forgive me or even blame them if they didn't, but I could apologize nonetheless. I could apologize to her closed door or shout it from the street if I had to. I wouldn't mention what happened to me at the Deliverance Center; it was liable to sound like another one of my "I'm changed" stories—Lord knows she's heard enough of those.

No, I'd just tell her I was sorry—sorry for all the pain I'd caused her and for the misery I brought upon her—and that I prayed that one day she'd forgive me. Then I'd be on my way. On my way to whatever God had in mind for me.

With that, my thoughts went back to the service and how it changed my perception of Jesus. It was as though I'd been looking at Him from a great distance all my life and was suddenly seeing Him up close. I could feel Him next to me, walking with me. His presence was more real and stronger than anything I ever felt—far stronger than the effects of any drug. I knew He was with me and because I knew I wasn't afraid. I felt curious and anxious but not afraid. His name alone had dispatched all fear and remedied all pain.

Pain.

I stopped suddenly, realizing for the first time that I wasn't in pain. I looked down...*at my feet.* They weren't hurting anymore. The awful agony that had been my constant companion for so long was gone. I couldn't remember when I stopped feeling the spikes stab into them with every step, couldn't recall when my every thought didn't focus on how much they hurt.

The pain was gone—completely gone.

I took a tentative step forward, half-expecting a harpoon of searing agony to rip into my footfall and shriek "April Fool!" more than halfway through the month. When nothing happened, I took another step and then another.

I clutched my Bible to my chest, lay my chin on its top edge, and closed my eyes thinking of what Pastor Kyle had whispered to me when I took his hand:

"The Hand of God is on your life, Mitchell. He calls you to His service. Don't be afraid."

I opened my eyes and crossed the street toward Martin Luther King Junior Memorial Park. From the sidewalk I could see across the entire park to the backyard of Momma's house.

My heart rejoiced as I headed into the park. I had to fight back the urge to run.

CHAPTER TWENTY-EIGHT

By the time I stood on the front porch of Momma's house I had braced myself for her every possible response to my appearance— or so I thought. I was not at all prepared for what she actually did: she opened the door while I was still knocking.

The last few times I came by, Momma had only peeked at me through the window and asked what I wanted, her flat refusal at the ready for whatever request I made. Once when I saw the drapes rustle and then settle, I knew it was Brenda who'd peeked and then gone to get Mom to do the honors.

I stood there looking dumb, my knuckles still poised where the door had been. I had expected to shout my apologies at the sealed building and suddenly I'm looking into my mother's face.

For what seemed a long time neither of us said anything; we just stood looking at each other. When it occurred to me that I should speak, I couldn't find the words. It felt as though a thousand years had passed between us. We'd been through so much, together and apart. For her the trials of life had started long before she even met my father. She had seen and known and survived suffering of a magnitude those pretenders I knew in the marines couldn't begin to imagine, let alone bear. She had known cruelty, betrayal, and abandonment and had struggled with loneliness and disappointment while fighting to keep her brood of ten from being overtaken and consumed by the world. And she'd had her demons too, demons she wrestled with and defeated for her family's sake, only to watch helplessly as her eldest child succumbed to his own. She'd prayed and cried and prayed again, beseeching her Father in Heaven to spare the life and save the soul of her foolish firstborn.

And now all I'd done to her, everything I'd put her through, came down on me with crushing force, and I stood speechless and ashamed on my mother's porch. The grand apology that had seemed so meaningful as I rehearsed it felt impotent and stupid now. How could I believe I could just drag my sorry self over here and make it all better with "I'm sorry"?

I thought to run, turn tail and catch the wind. It would have been better if she hadn't opened the door, better if I'd had to shout my apology from the street and at least believe I'd done something noble and self-redeeming. Better if I hadn't had to face her.

Momma's gaze went from my face to the Bible in my hands and back. I couldn't even guess what she was thinking, but there was something in my mother's eyes—her dark, wise old eyes that brought comfort and hope to my spirit.

And I realized that Jesus was with Momma too; He'd been with her all along. He'd protected and kept her through loss and longing and loneliness. He'd carried her through the storms that life—and her son—had brought upon her.

He, Jesus, had seen her through it all. Momma had put her hope in Him, drawn her strength from Him. Just as His Hand was on my life, it had always been on hers.

Without a word Momma stood back, opening the door wider, so that I could enter her house at 28 Bond Street.

CHAPTER TWENTY-NINE

I'd been in the house all of ten minutes when Momma raised the subject of me going into rehab. We were in the kitchen; Brenda and I were seated across from each other at the table while Mom made coffee. Mom was the consummate multitasker: she could brew a perfect pot of Mountain Roast while simultaneously throwing me for a loop without spilling a drop.

I can't describe how deflated I felt. I didn't want to go into another program, didn't want to be subjected to another "recovery" format composed of meetings, addiction education, and "sharing" sessions led by facilitators whose only legitimate claim to the title "counselor" was their own addiction and whose greatest success after twenty years of sobriety was that they hadn't gotten high in twenty years.

I wanted nothing more to do with programs. Programs were for junkies, and I wasn't a junkie anymore. I was… actually, I didn't know what I was; God hadn't revealed that to me yet. It had only been an hour or so since I gave myself over to Him. In my heart I knew He had a plan for me. I knew it as certainly as Pastor Kyle and Chaplain Tommy had known, knew it as sure as—many years before them—my baby sister Stephanie had known.

"You know Alonzo's there," Brenda said. "Been there almost a month. He loves it, says it's a good program." It was good to be on speaking terms with Brenda again. We were alike in so many ways. We'd both seen the inside of "the belly of the beast," the darkest and most desperate underside of drug culture. We'd both suffered life-threatening injuries via knife attacks and had brushes with the law that often resulted in incarceration. But Brenda had beaten her demons. She'd gotten it together long before I was released from prison. For the last several years she'd been working as a caregiver in a retirement facility while studying for her degree in nursing. A mother of four and just a year and five days my junior, Brenda had come a long way. Sometimes I wonder if I resented Brenda more for the way she so casually succeeded in her recovery (no muss, no fuss, and no programs) than for the way she came between Momma and me while I was running.

"Depending on how soon you went in, Alonzo said you could be in the same phase group as him," Brenda offered, as an incentive, I suppose. Alonzo, our nephew, was the son of Brenda's twin brother, Michael. Mike had also had addiction issues and had also gotten clean before I got out of Rahway. Unfortunately, however, his recovery had not come soon enough to help Mike stop his son from falling into the same trap of drug abuse. Alonzo, in his twenties now, was barely a teenager when I was incarcerated. I remember him as a bright, good-looking boy with amazing green eyes—bound to mature to lady-killer adulthood.

Without realizing it, I had managed to stop hating the idea of me going into rehab long enough to hate the idea that it had been necessary for Alonzo. A member of the next generation of my family, Alonzo deserved a far better inheritance than the legacy of addiction his elders had left him.

They all did.

I have roughly twenty nieces and nephews, courtesy of six of my siblings, but am myself childless. The gods of addiction had caught me early, held me interminably, and released me reluctantly. I'm glad to say all my nieces and nephews love me, and I'm crazy about all of them. I was a pretty good uncle when I was clean: loving, giving, and generous. It's one of my greatest regrets that I had no offspring of my own to add to their ranks. I think I could have made a fine dad—except for the thirty years of addiction, I mean.

"You can call for a phone interview tomorrow," Momma said, handing me a cup of coffee. I had declined her offer of dinner as that massive meal I'd had at the Deliverance Center hadn't even begun to fade. "I have the number. The director's name is Phil."

I took the cup from Momma without meeting her gaze directly. I didn't want to discourage her with what she'd pick up during eye contact. Evidently she hadn't been speaking in general when she asked if I'd go into rehab the last few times I came to the house; she'd had a specific program in mind. I sipped my coffee and thought about how deeply I detested the notion of yet another rehab. I knew rehabs; I'd *run* a rehab. I wanted nothing more to do with a philosophy of recovery without cure. I didn't want to submit to an environment where the only certainty was that I would always be an addict. I had come to Momma's to make amends, to restore the broken fellowship between my family and me and maybe even convince them somehow that I was through with drugs. How could I make her understand that going into rehab again would be contrary, a threat to the newly restored me?

I went running to God in my mind. I had only a little while ago made the decision to put my life in His hands. Could His plan for me really include another program?

"Hello, my name is Mitch and I'm... I'm..."

What, Lord? What am I?

Quietly and desperately I cried out for the Jesus I knew was with and in me, asking Him for revelation, some sign of His design. Did He want me to do this?

The kitchen fell silent around me. I hadn't noticed when Brenda and Momma stopped talking to watch me. I was preoccupied with "prayer."

I looked at my mother and sister as I tried to reason out my feelings. Should I tell them what happened to me at the Deliverance Center? Would they understand that I belonged to God now and didn't need another program? After all, they were both believers in the gospel—would they believe that I now believed?

And if they did—then what? Where would I go from there? For a walk to the unemployment office or a romp through the want ads? Did the Lord want me to sleep on Momma's couch while polishing fenders at the Jiffy Car Wash until He was ready to use me? No, I wasn't feeling that.

There was no arguing the fact that currently I was a mess: undernourished, grungy, and broke. As it was I couldn't even prove I existed—not officially. During this last relapse I had managed to lose every document proving I'd been born, served my country, or held a job. Rehabs, for all I hated about them, were good for helping one get his paperwork and health back in order. I suppose a recovery program was as good a place as any to get back in shape—and get legit again—while I waited on God. And adding up my time in recovery while reinforcing my basic knowledge of the practices for maintaining my sobriety was not automatically a bad thing.

But no program, however accredited or professional would make me believe I was not healed, forever free of addiction. No counselor, no peer group—no rehab would ever make me a junkie again.

I looked at the two women watching me expectantly. I couldn't tell what Momma was thinking; her expression gave nothing away. I guess life had taught her to wait and see. You couldn't beat Momma for patience. She could watch a glacier migrate if she had to. Maybe it was that more than anything else that convinced me. I'd do the program and not speak of my epiphany at the Deliverance Center. I'd hold off telling her about my newfound relationship with Jesus until I had more to offer than just talk.

I let the idea settle inside my acceptance, thinking maybe God did want me to do this—for Momma. It would make her happy and give her much-needed peace of mind. Maybe my first job on this road to wherever Jesus was leading me was to learn to consider someone's feelings other than my own.

I looked into Momma's eyes and nodded.

"Okay, Mom, I'll call tomorrow," I promised.

Momma walked over and kissed my sunken, unshaven cheek.

"Okay." She smiled. "Now get your butt in that shower while I find something for you to wear. You stink, boy!"

"Amen!" Brenda laughed. I raised my cup to my lips to hide my smile. Despite my anxiety, my sister's laughter was a good sound.

CHAPTER THIRTY

The next morning after breakfast, I got Phil's number from Mom and called for my phone screening. I pretended not to notice her pleasure for not having to come to me. It felt good.

I kept zoning out during my conversation with the program's resident director. My mind drifted from my die-hard distaste for the thought of going into rehab despite my acceptance to wondering about all the prophesies I'd heard over the years concerning my inevitable service to God; so my focus on the questions coming from my interviewer was dim at best. Fortunately I'd done one or two such screenings; I knew the information Phil required even before he asked: drug abuse history, whether or not I needed detoxification (the program didn't want to take in a client who was liable to spend his first night in their custody climbing the walls with violent withdrawal), my current legal status (they didn't want to be accused of harboring a fugitive from the law either), my finances, and the present state of my health.

While questioning me about outlaw connections or gang affiliations, Phil mentioned he knew that Alonzo and I were related and wanted to know if our being there together might create a conflict. I understood his concern: family members who share substance abuse issues often also share great mutual hostility stemming from the fact that they'd had occasion to cheat or rob each other. The twin brothers I mentioned earlier who attacked and robbed people together eventually ended up dead together. The official cause of death was accidental overdose; street gossip, however, held that one had accidentally contaminated his portion of a package they shared while attempting to poison the other. I didn't go to the funeral but was told it was a largely attended spectacle. Apparently the untimely death of twin siblings was a morbid attraction of considerable magnitude. I assured Phil that there was no ill will between Alonzo and me. I loved my nephew.

Between questions about my misspent life, Phil told me about the program, its different phases, restrictions, duration, and so on. I really wasn't listening. It was just another program to me. I was taken aback when Phil told me that the format took an entire year to complete (that I did hear!) I thought about a program I went through in Newark back in '80. Known as a hardcore TC (therapeutic community), their recovery format was grounded in the appalling conviction that drug addicts were absolute losers, the bottom-feeders of society. Once an addict, always an addict, they maintained; the addict's only redeeming quality being that he didn't have to succumb to the urge to use (that actually made sense to me then). I remember being shouted at and cursed at regularly and being made to wear handwritten signs around my neck for violating one of their scores of infractions—signs that read "I am a thief" or "I can't accept constructive criticism, ask me why." Once I was subjected to group ridicule because another client (they called us "patients") didn't like my nose. That program, too, had a duration of one year. Believe it or not, I didn't wash out for ten months.

Lord!

I was ruminating on that repulsive memory even as Phil was winding up the interview. I barely heard his last question and asked him to repeat it.

"I said, when can you come in?"

The question, though expected, still managed to catch me off guard.

"How about tomorrow?" I asked.

"How about *today*?" Phil countered and again I'm caught flat-footed. I'd never known a program to take in clients so soon after the initial screening. With most there was at least a week or more before a bed was available. This place must be really hard up for clients or patients or forever-addicts or whatever.

"Well..." I stalled, "I have to pack... find someone to drive me..." and I wondered, *drive me where?* I don't know the name of this place or its location.

Phil consented. "Tomorrow, then, but don't bring a lot of stuff. And come sober." Then he hung up, leaving me to stare resentfully at the phone in my hand.

Come sober? Why would I go into rehab high?

Yeah, like I hadn't done it before.

CHAPTER THIRTY-ONE

The next morning, Tuesday, April 21, 2004, I left for the Market Street Mission in Morristown, New Jersey.

Momma hugged and kissed her middle-aged son as though he were a nervous five-year-old on his first day at kindergarten. As I stepped out on the porch, she took my hand, pressing a twenty-dollar bill into my palm.

"For cigarettes," she said, and there was that hopeful sparkle in her wise dark eyes again that made me wish I felt more positive about going to this rehab. I smiled just the same and promised to call her as soon as the rules permitted. I kissed her cheek and told her I'd be all right. I think she believed me; more importantly I know *I* believed me. I'd spent much of the rest of yesterday following my phone screening in prayer: sitting alone in the dining room, looking out the window into the backyard and asking God if this was the right thing to do. I don't know if I expected an answer, but I had no doubt that He was close to me, that He was listening. It isn't easy to explain except to say that in spite of the anxiety I felt, there was a reassuring peace with me that drove away true fear. I wasn't afraid, thank God, but I wished there was some way I could know His plan, where He was taking me.

As afternoon wore into evening, I decided it didn't matter.

Whatever God wanted of me, for me, with me, I'd learn when He was ready for me to know. I knew that whatever He had in mind was far better than anything I'd come up with on my own. As for this rehab, it wouldn't kill me and it certainly wouldn't make me a junkie again, so I won't sweat over it anymore. I can do this. I can do this for Momma.

I climbed into the backseat of Brenda's Lexus with the new clothes and toiletries she and Momma bought for me last night. Debbie, Alonzo's mother, sat up front to give directions while Brenda drove. Momma stood on the porch and returned my wave as we pulled off. Her smile conveyed both sadness and joy; hope and unshakable faith glistened in her eyes.

Except for Fritz, none of my six brothers were there to see me off. I couldn't blame them for not wanting to miss work for this. I'd been one sorry excuse for a big brother for a very long time, not there to protect or support any of them since I could remember. The last time I shared something decent or life-sustaining with them, the last adult interaction we'd had that wasn't overshadowed by my addiction, was tucked away in some obscure memory shamefully far back in the past. They all had their own lives now. They pretty much had to grow up without me. I thought of them during my prayer time yesterday and was overcome with regret. If I could have one more chance, I promised God, even this late in my life, I'd come back a big brother they could respect and admire.

Admittedly I didn't know what I was doing with this whole "prayer thing." I was feeling my way along in this newfound fellowship with God, playing it as it came. I didn't know what to say to Him or ask of Him. I wanted so much, and it seemed the more I could feel Him with me, the more I wanted. I did know that there was more to being with Him than just submitting my laundry list of requests. But I'd lost so much time and blown so many opportunities. Part of me screamed for a chance to get it all back, to reverse every betrayed trust and reclaim every squandered gift. I couldn't help it—the wanting.

As Brenda piloted the car onto Route 206 north for Morristown, the faces of my brothers blended among the images of missed chances filling my mind. I felt heartsick and ashamed, but at the same time my resolve knew increased strength. *I can do this*, I told myself. *I can do this for them: my brothers.*

Up front, Brenda and Debbie were chattering away, oblivious of the silent vows being made in the backseat. I always liked Debbie. Although divorced from Michael several years, the two had remained close friends and not just for Alonzo's sake; I guess they just got along better as exes. Thinking of their aborted marriage made me think about the failure of my own. It had been awhile since I saw or even thought about Debra, just one more person who would have been better off without my gods-driven presence in her life.

Lord. So much to atone for; so many amends to make. Can a man be so wrong—responsible for so much hurt and harm—and still serve You? Can You really want someone as corrupt and broken as me?

The senior pastor at my mother's church said that God loves a contrite spirit and a broken heart. As we drove farther into unfamiliar territory (I'd never traveled to North Jersey before), I concluded this had to be true because too many of us don't think of God at all *until* we're broken, lying smashed and useless at the bottom of our lives. For many, a real relationship with Jesus means first ruining every other relationship. They—we—call on Him only after we've sunk so low that no human ability can dredge us up. We're beyond needful, even beyond desperate; we have to believe or die. That God should want us at all is beyond comprehension, more than any human being has a right to even hope for.

"You okay back there?" Brenda asked, breaking into my reverie.

Our eyes met in the rearview mirror, and I nodded at my younger sister.

"I'm good."

She smiled and turned her attention back to the road and to her navigator. Brenda had been my number-one nemesis for much of this last year of my insanity. She'd been there to castigate me whenever I came to the house and even admonishing Momma for giving me so much as a piece of bread to munch on. One night in late March when Momma refused to let me in, I stayed out on the porch all night. It had been cold, but I'd suffered worse. The idea was for Momma to find me out there in the morning, shivering from exposure, and take me in.

The only hitch to my otherwise ingenious scheme was that it wasn't Momma who found me; it was Brenda. Needless to say she was not overcome with guilt or remorse. She cursed me six ways from Sunday, called me names that would make a merchant marine cry, and sped off to work in her car—and Momma still wouldn't let me in.

And now this woman—this younger sister of mine who wanted nothing to do with me just days ago—had spent her own money to help buy clothing and toiletries for me. She'd taken a day off from her job to make sure I made it to rehab. She'd gone well out of her way to help me.

I turned from Brenda to look out the window at the passing scenery, overcome with gratitude. My resolve was further reinforced.

I can do this, I vowed. *I can do this for Brenda.*

I didn't know what to make of Morristown as we entered the city commons—which I found anything but common. The place was very neat, expensive looking, a minimetropolis. I could barely count the number of businesses spread over such a brief area. At the very heart of downtown rested an attractive park that took up a city block, known as "The Green." I was hard-pressed to imagine a single business that wasn't represented in the four blocks surrounding it or on the outlying avenues: Starbucks, Subway Sandwiches, and Chinese and Italian take-out; Godiva Chocolates, Century Twenty-One, and Filene's department stores; a Foot Locker and a Lady Foot Locker; The Gap, Dunkin Donuts, and Burger King; at least two bakeries; Omaha Steaks, Baskin-Robbins, and maybe a dozen restaurants catering to every taste from Indian to urban; no fewer than four major bank branches and a handful of dry cleaners, tailor shops, and hardware and package goods stores.

What I found even more impressive was that our destination apparently was in the midst of all the commerce. Debbie was directing Brenda to circle the block on the south side of The Green, as the rehab was a one-way street. I was looking right into the heart of the park as we pulled to a stop and debarked.

I stood frozen in place for a long moment, mouth open and staring, unable to process what I was seeing.

The Market Street Mission was an unremarkable, four-storied structure of tan-and-white brick. The tinted glass double doors on the left side of the building were locked, allowing neither entrance nor egress of the building. Access was gained only through the single clear glass door several feet to the right of those...

A door positioned under a huge electronic cross proclaiming "Jesus Saves" in blue-and-yellow neon.

I looked at my sisters (despite her divorce from my brother, the family still referred to Debbie as "Sis"), my face a mask of bewilderment.

This is a rehab?

If the women saw my confusion, they didn't let on they had. Brenda took my bag from the car and then took my arm as Debbie opened the door to the Market Street Mission. Inside the foyer the entire wall near the elevator was a red brick-face honorarium recognizing the financial support of individuals, groups, and companies sponsoring the mission. I instantly recognized the name Kent Manahan, a news anchor from the New Jersey News Network. Several other names on the display I at least found familiar.

Four steps took us up from street level to the first-floor reception desk manned by whom I presumed were two program clients doing desk duty. One was reading a John Grisham novel while the other fielded incoming calls. The reader looked up from the paperback and nodded as we approached.

"Help you?"

"Yeah, I..." I couldn't immediately remember why I was there. I was floored by the place—by the very *idea* of the place. The question: *This is a rehab?* kept circling in my head. I'd never seen a Christian drug rehab—never even *heard* of one. At the far right of the desk, double doors gave entrance to what was obviously a church sanctuary: a stage at its far end housed a wooden pulpit at its center and a wooden cross large enough to actually crucify a man upon in its left corner. A hand-painted mural on the wall behind me presented men with emaciated frames, scruffy clothing and solemn, troubled faces. Broken, lost men. One of them appeared to be reaching toward the Bible verse painted in script on a white portion of the same wall:

> *Therefore, if anyone is in Christ, he is a new creation;*
> *the old has gone, the new has come!*
> II Corinthians 5:17

I read that verse over and over, its significance resonating in my spirit before realizing the desk man was still waiting to hear what I wanted. I turned to see Brenda was already informing him that I was a new intake with an appointment to see Phil.

"He's downstairs in the dining room," the client/receptionist told us. "He'll be right up—or you can go down and have lunch with the house, if you want."

Brenda—no doubt eager to hit the road for the hour's drive back to Trenton—declined with thanks. I said no as well. Mom had seen to it I had a massive breakfast before leaving Bond Street. Debbie also turned down the lunch invitation but didn't appear in a hurry to leave. She was hoping to get a glimpse of Alonzo.

"Well, you can have a seat if you want," the desk man offered, pointing to a long bench that was actually a church pew taking up most of the wall to the right of the sanctuary in a narrow hallway. More to avoid obstructing traffic around the reception desk than out of a need to sit down, the three of us walked over and took a seat.

"You all right, Mitchell?" Brenda asked, putting her hand over mine. I looked at her and nodded. The truth was I was flabbergasted by my surroundings. *A Christian rehab?* A drug and alcohol addiction program that included God?

"You Alonzo's uncle?"

The question came from a door leading to the upper floors of the building. I looked over to see a bald, heavy-set black man about my age, who I assumed was Phil, the guy who had done my phone screening.

"Yeah," I answered, getting to my feet.

The big guy eyed me critically and growled, "I don't want any stuff out of you."

I stared, unsure what to say. Then the big man grinned and walked toward us, his hand extended in greeting. "Manning."

I gave him my name and shook his hand. Debbie moved in close to us and whispered, "Where's Alonzo?"

"You just missed him," Manning told her. "The van just left to take the afternoon shift to the warehouse."

Clearly disappointed, Debbie looked at the door through which

Manning had come; perhaps hoping Alonzo would appear there despite being told he would not. Although she probably would have been prohibited from speaking with her son outside permitted visiting days, she had hoped for a chance to at least see him.

"I'll let him know you were here," Manning said, for whatever consolation he thought that was worth. Debbie nodded her thanks.

"Mitch?"

At the sound of my name, my sisters and I turned. A short, bespectacled man of about sixty stood at the reception desk, addressing us.

"Are you Mitch?" he repeated. He was a soft-spoken man, his voice slightly raspy, the voice of a man who had smoked many years. I left the women and walked over to meet him.

"Yes, I'm Mitch." I was still enthralled with this incredibly untraditional rehab I had entered but recovered enough to communicate. "Are you Phil?"

"Phil Dosier," the resident director said, holding out his hand. "You all set?"

I shook hands with him, a multitude of questions spinning in my head. "I'm ready."

"Chaplain?" the desk man who had been taking calls said to Phil. Phil turned toward him.

"Yeah?"

"Phone, Chap," the other answered. "Says it's important."

"I'll take it in my office," Phil told him, and then he turned to me. "Be with you in a minute, Mitch."

"Chaplain?" I heard myself ask. "You're a chaplain?"

"That's me," Phil Dosier replied. He then made a half turn to leave and halted, probably sensing I had another question to ask. "Something wrong?"

"This rehab," I said, choosing my words as carefully as I could, "is Christian?"

Both desk men looked at me with amused smiles. Phil was smiling too, but in a way that put me completely at ease. "As Christian as it gets. I'm sure I mentioned that during your screening yesterday."

I was sure he did too—during my rehab-resenting zone-outs. "Yeah, you did. Guess I forgot."

Chaplain Phil Dosier's smile relaxed and he eyed me with concern. "Is that a problem for you?"

Something bright and ticklishly alive ignited in my belly. I don't know if the smile I felt inside showed on my face. "No, Chaplain—no problem."

"Good," he said as he walked behind the desk toward a door that evidently led to his office. "Be right back."

A moment later Brenda and Debbie came over to tell me they were leaving.

"Take care, brother-in-law," Debbie said giving me a hug. "Give Alonzo my love."

"I will," I told her. "Thanks for coming with us, Sis."

Brenda hugged me, kissed my cheek, and brushed a bit of lint or something off my new shirt. When she wasn't condemning my behavior, my sister was correcting my appearance.

"You'll be all right, big brother," she said and hugged me again. I hugged her back, thanking her with my whole heart as I wished her a safe drive home.

Both sisters blew kisses as they exited the building, sparking chuckles from passersby. Not in the least embarrassed, I waved until the door closed behind them. Then I took in this place, this Market Street Mission.

And I knew I would be all right, knew far beyond the vows I made and remade and then made again as we journeyed here. Jesus was with me. He had heard my anguished cries from my basement tomb, taken the rocks from my hands, removed the sores from my feet, and expelled the evil gods from my soul.

Jesus was with me. He'd been with me all along, delivered me out of my insanity and into this place, this place of healing and recovery.

Jesus was with me. He had not only come here *with* me; He was waiting here *for* me. I still didn't know exactly what His plan was for me, but I knew now He wanted me to be here.

While I waited for Chaplain Phil Dosier's return, I studied that Bible verse from II Corinthians on the foyer wall.

Therefore, if anyone is in Christ, he is a new creation; the old has gone, the new has come!

A new creation. The words implanted themselves in my spirit like a seedling, like a wonderful promise. I knew that in this house no one would try to make me believe that I was still a junkie, doomed to live and function and even prosper in the shadow of relapse.

I would need never fear the gods of addiction again—not ever again.

My heart felt near to bursting with joy. *Yes,* I thought as I felt the Spirit of the Lord embrace me, *I can do this program, this Market Street Mission rehab.*

I can do it for me.

CHAPTER THIRTY-TWO

"I'd like a copy of that, Mitch," the class instructor said as I concluded my reading. I looked up from my testimony—the essay assignment we were given—to the rather impressed expressions on the faces of my classmates.

Classmates. I'm still amazed to call them that. When I walked into this place—this Market Street Mission almost eight years ago I didn't imagine that the life from which I'd been delivered would be a source of enlightenment and inspiration for so many people: not just those who, like me, had known the curse of addiction but people who had never so much as taken a drink. People I never would have believed I'd be privileged to be in fellowship with, people I never imagined I'd be blessed to call my friends.

The years following my entrance to the Market Street Mission have been abundant with blessings. A graduation ceremony was held for my class of thirteen who had completed the Life Change Program in April 2005 (looking back I notice that April has been an eventful month in my life). One of the local churches volunteered their sanctuary for the event. Alonzo and I took the honor walk together and the audience of family and friends who had attended the event included at least twenty of Alonzo's and my relatives. When my name was called and I went to receive my certificate of completion, I looked out over the sea of faces of people who had suffered through their loved ones' addiction. I thanked the mission staff member who handed me my certificate and accepted my share of applause. My mother and siblings were not hard to spot among the crowd; their support and pride was very energetic and quite vocal. I wanted to shout and cheer with them, shout about the change that had taken place in me over the last year, shout that I was a new person, forever dedicated to serving God. Even if I'd been permitted to say more than thank you, however, I couldn't have found the words. Looking at Momma's face (as distinctive among that crowd as her voice would be in a noisy stadium), I could see I didn't need the words. She knew.

Immediately after graduation I was accepted into the mission's Leadership Training Program. I was on fire to find my place in God's plan and begin the work He had in mind for me. I had no idea what that plan was but was satisfied that leadership was as good a place as any to start looking. My role was essentially to be an example to new program members that the system works, to head work crews and chair recovery meetings, and to "grow in my faith," as then-program-director George Moussab put it; that is, to increase in my knowledge of God's word through worship, study, and fellowship with other believers.

The Market Street Mission is to conventional rehabs what Home Depot is to the local dollar store. While its Life Change Program employs such therapeutic concepts as working the principles of Narcotics Anonymous and Alcoholics Anonymous, including attending their meetings—useful tools for recovery—the mission teaches that true healing is about transformation and renewal, placing my life in God's hands and allowing Him to lead me. I learned that victory over addiction is not about having the strength to resist temptation; it's about leaning on the One who does have the strength.

The mission uses all the treatment techniques found in other recovery houses, paying great respect for the steps and principles of NA and AA. The difference is that while other programs focus on recovery, at the Market Street Mission the focus is on life. Recovering addicts recover; new creations in Christ live.

As a leadership trainee I received a stipend of twenty dollars a week. The mission took care of meals and my living expenses, of course. By then I couldn't have been less concerned about money. The mission provided an education in the Word of God comparable to that of any Bible College or divinity school (I know that because a staff member enrolled in a local Christian college once took me to school with her when I expressed an interest in becoming a preacher).

Eventually I was allowed to stand in the pulpit and deliver the message at chapel service once a month. I remember how nervous I was that first time. I made an attempt to preach the sermon I'd written from memory. I didn't do very well; I stuttered, rifled through my notes, and repeated myself. Afterward, a program member congratulated me, commenting that my message made the Bible passage from which I'd preached understandable. He even called me "Reverend." I was exhilarated.

I was still in the leadership program when I met Cordelia, the cousin of a former classmate of mine; I was a staff member and chaplain when we married in 2008. It had been Mr. David Scott, the executive director of the mission, who suggested I enroll for the chaplaincy. He'd been a constant source of inspiration and support to me almost from the start. As I began to improve as a preacher, Mr. Scott arranged with the pastors of area churches to have me address their congregations. He said I was a good advertisement for what the mission could accomplish in a man's life. Apart from the mission client who called me "Reverend," it was the greatest compliment anyone had ever paid me.

I like being a chaplain. I've been called many things; chaplain's the best. Cordelia sometimes teases me as I hang my badge around my neck in preparation for a ministry assignment. She says I look like a cop. I can only shake my head and smile in response. No one has ever mistaken me for a cop.

I like Cordelia. She has a good sense of humor and a sweet smile. If there was one thing I feared I wouldn't get, it's a second chance to be a husband. Thank God I'm not blessed according to what I deserve.

In all honesty, it has not been a flawless, trouble-free transition from where I was to where I am. I've had my bad days. Old behaviors and attitudes have revisited to threaten and erase the progress I've made. Fear, doubt, and memories of the man I was show up to mock and taunt me time and again, and most certainly I've made mistakes. Thankfully God has placed people in my life who regard me with compassion and patience, forgiving my faults and encouraging the man I'm trying to be.

Again blessed well beyond anything I merit.

Sometimes I feel just a little bit cheated that I didn't get to watch the gods of addiction die. I revisit that day—that very moment at the Deliverance Center when they were inside me screaming in terror and squirming in unbearable pain as the Son of the Living God enveloped, embraced, and filled me. I remember enjoying their suffering, leaning toward it, reveling in it, trying to taste their hellish demise with all my senses and instincts.

But I was distracted—by Pastor Kyle, I think. When I thought to look again, they were gone—already dead, I guess. Or maybe they weren't dead. Maybe Jesus doesn't work that way. I've still so much to learn about Him. I read the rest of the story about the demon-possessed man. Jesus didn't kill his demons; He merely sent them away. Maybe He did likewise with my gods, moved them out as He moved in. I'm good with that, I really am. Still, I sometimes regret that I didn't get to watch it happening.

And I'm still looking for my place in God's plan, seeking to realize His design for my life. Sometimes I think I'm close to an answer. I reach the peak of one mountain only to see Him beckoning to me from the summit of another. I never get tired or feel discouraged, though. I feel elated, invigorated. With Him I anticipate the trials and challenges of life with hope and gratefulness. With Jesus every day brings victory.

Oh, I almost forgot: the sores on my feet never returned. All traces of affliction, the infection, the pain are gone. It's as though nothing had ever been wrong with them. I walk, I run, I dance with Cordelia, and occasionally when I'm in the mood to hear her sweet laugh, I dance *for* Cordelia. With understandable exceptions I'm as healthy as I was as a young marine, and in some very important ways I'm far healthier. There's a story in the Bible about a man who couldn't walk until he met Jesus …

And I move on. I press on, as the apostle said, to what's ahead. Recently I've been assigned as spiritual leader at the newly opened Jersey Shore Rescue Mission in Asbury Park: a homeless shelter and soup kitchen plus an intake headquarters for the men of a whole new community seeking to enter the Market Street Mission. I'm on the ground floor of a new ministry, reaching out with God's hand to the least, the last, the lost of Monmouth County. I return to Market Street often to pick up supplies for the Jersey Shore Mission. I still preach there at morning service once a month and I attend an advanced Bible study once a week. It was at this study where my instructor, Pastor Peter Amerman, assigned us to write and read our personal testimonies. I wrote about the life out of which Jesus delivered me. I wrote about the opportunities I missed or abused, the years I squandered, the loved ones I hurt.

I wrote about the gods of addiction.

"Amazing testimony," Pastor Pete remarked as I concluded my reading. "And you refer to addiction as a spirit. A god."

Around the room the pastor's sentiment was evidently shared by the other class members, including my boss Mr. Scott. I was simultaneously moved and surprised by their reaction. Surely someone else had seen, known, talked about the gods?

I handed him the copy (I'd made five) of my testimony as he'd requested. He gripped my hand with immense affection. "I'd like to read this in my class, if you don't mind."

In addition to pastoring at one of the local churches, Pastor Pete also facilitated one of the advanced second-phase recovery classes at the mission. The idea of my testimony being used as a means of helping men in recovery honored and humbled me. I told him to by all means use it any way he deemed appropriate.

"You should expand on this," the pastor suggested. I had no idea what he meant.

"Expand?" I asked. "Expand how?"

"Take it a step further," the pastor explained. "This is a powerful and unique testimony to the power of God to redeem. And it offers a view of addiction that many people might find helpful. This is the stuff that saves lives and wins souls for the Lord."

Saving lives and winning souls, I thought, excited. Wouldn't *that* be something?

"Write about it, Mitch," Pastor Pete urged. "Write about your life, your struggles, and your victory through Christ. Write about your views on addiction as the spirit at the heart of the disease. Write about the gods of addiction, and let the world read about it."

Other members of the class agreed wholeheartedly with Pastor Pete's suggestion. I looked over the faces of my classmates and nodded.

"Maybe I will," I said.

And so I have and that, dear reader brings this story to a close. I thank you for spending this time with me. If this work has been helpful to someone struggling with addiction, I am grateful. I always wanted to write something that someone would find important. In my heart I feel I've done that here; I just didn't know I'd have to live it first.

Writing this has only compelled me to write more. I've still so much to say about the gods of addiction. As a matter of fact, there's something knocking on the door of my heart even as I wrap this up…

One last thing: I'm being ordained as an associate pastor at my church in Paterson this year in—you guessed it—April.

Maybe this is what God had in mind for me all along—or maybe He just had to adjust His plan to compensate for my thick-headedness and bad decisions. I'm certain now that I was meant to serve Him just as my baby sister and others had prophesied. Falling into addiction was a choice I made, but maybe He decided to use my choice to qualify me to fight His battle in this particular arena. I don't know. I've a great deal of learning to do. But I do know about the power of the gods of addiction to destroy lives, and the power of God to save them.

Several times during the telling of this story, I paused to identify myself. It seems now a most appropriate way to end this writing.

My name is Mitch—Chaplain Mitchell Green—and I am a new creation in Christ.

TO GOD BE THE GLORY!